Enabling Technologies for Petaflops Computing

Series Foreword

The world of modern computing potentially offers many helpful methods and tools to scientists and engineers, but the fast pace of change in computer hardware, software, and algorithms often makes practical use of the newest computing technology difficult. The Scientific and Engineering Computation series focuses on rapid advances in computing technologies and attempts to facilitate transferring these technologies to applications in science and engineering. It will include books on theories, methods, and original applications in such areas as parallelism, large-scale simulations, time-critical computing, computer-aided design and engineering, use of computers in manufacturing, visualization of scientific data, and human-machine interface technology.

The series will help scientists and engineers to understand the current world of advanced computation and to anticipate future developments that will impact their computing environments and open up new capabilities and modes of computation.

This book documents the findings of the Workshop on Enabling Technologies for Petaflops Computing, which was held in February 1994. The key objectives of the workshop were:

(1) identifying applications requiring Petaflops performance,
(2) assessing the technologies needed for achieving Petaflops computing systems,
(3) establishing fundamental research issues, and
(4) recommending a near-term research agenda.

The book has been written with the two readership categories in mind: technology policy makers and researchers, who are interested in understanding the challenges of achieving Petaflops computing and in defining research programs leading to this goal.

Janusz S. Kowalik

Enabling Technologies for Petaflops Computing

Thomas Sterling, Paul Messina, and Paul H. Smith

The MIT Press
Cambridge, Massachusetts
London, England

© 1995 Massachusetts Institute of Technology

All rights reserved. No part of this book may be reproduced in any form by any electronic or mechanical means (including photocopying, recording, or information storage and retrieval) without permission in writing from the publisher.

This book was set by the authors and was printed and bound in the United States of America.

Library of Congress Cataloging-in-Publication Data

Sterling, Thomas Lawrence.
 Enabling technologies for Petaflops computing / Thomas Sterling, Paul Messina, and Paul H. Smith.
   p.   cm.—(Scientific and engineering computation)
 Includes bibliographical references.
 ISBN 0-262-69176-0 (alk. paper)
  1. Petaflops computers. I. Messina, P. C. (Paul C.), 1943–   . II. Smith, Paul H., 1943–   . III. Title. IV. Series.
QA76.885.S74   1995
004.2'51—dc20   95-15978
                                                                                      CIP

Contents

	Preface	ix
1	**Introduction**	**1**
1.1	Overview	1
1.2	Objectives	3
1.3	Approach	4
1.4	Background	6
1.5	Technical Challenges	9
2	**Petaflops from Two Perspectives**	**13**
2.1	Seymour Cray Keynote Address	13
2.2	Konstantin Likharev Keynote Address	17
3	**Summary of Working Group Reports**	**27**
3.1	Applications	27
3.2	Device Technology	29
3.3	Architecture	35
3.4	Software Technology	40
4	**Applications Working Group**	**45**
4.1	Introduction	45
4.2	Applications Motivation	45
4.3	Issues/Characteristics for Architecture	51
4.4	Exemplar Applications	54
4.5	Algorithmic Issues	72
4.6	Acknowledgments	74
5	**Device Technology Working Group: Semiconductor, Optical, and Superconductive Devices**	**75**
5.1	Introduction	75
5.2	Silicon Device Technology	75

5.3	Optical Devices	83
5.4	Projections for Technology Development	89
5.5	Optical Technology	93
5.6	Future R&D in Optics	97
5.7	Superconductive Electronics	99
5.8	Device Technology Summary	106
5.9	Acknowledgments	107

6 Architecture Working Group: Architecture and Systems — 109

6.1	Metrics and Limitations	111
6.2	Petaflops Architectures Design Points	114
6.3	Role of Device Technology	120
6.4	Obstacles and Uncertainties	124
6.5	Final Comments	127
6.6	Acknowledgments	128

7 Software Technology Working Group: System Software and Tools — 129

7.1	Introduction	129
7.2	The Challenge of Software Technology	130
7.3	Trends and Opportunities	132
7.4	BLISS versus the Metasystem	134
7.5	Discussion of Software Technology Areas	137
7.6	Recommendations	145
7.7	Software Technology Conclusions	149
7.8	Acknowledgments	150

8 Major Findings — 153

8.1	Summary Position	153
8.2	Feasibility	153
8.3	Broad Potential Use	154

8.4	Cost is a Pacing Item	154
8.5	Manageable Reliability	154
8.6	MIMD Model	155
8.7	Latency Management and Parallelism	155
8.8	Riding the Semiconductor Technology Wave	156
8.9	Memory	156
8.10	Software Paradigm Shift	157
8.11	Merging of Technologies	158
8.12	A Role for Superconductivity	158
8.13	Optical Logic Unlikely	158

9 Issues and Implications   159

9.1	Why Consider Petaflops Now?	159
9.2	Role of a Petaflops Computer	160
9.3	Side-effect Products	161
9.4	Impact of Exotic Technologies	161
9.5	Performance Versus Efficiency	163
9.6	Programming Paradigms	163
9.7	U.S. Capabilities in Memory Fabrication	164
9.8	Special Widgets, Where to Invest	165
9.9	A Range of Architectures	165
9.10	Far-side Architectures	166
9.11	Latency Hiding Techniques	167
9.12	Long versus Short Latency Machines	167
9.13	SIA Predictions	168
9.14	I/O Scaling	168

10 Recommendations and Conclusions   171

10.1	Recommendations for Initiatives	171
10.2	Concluding Observations	173

A	**Attendee List**	177
	Bibliography	179

Preface

Petaflops is a measure of computer performance equal to a million billion operations (or floating point operations) per second. It is comparable to more than ten times all the networked computing capability in the U.S. and is ten thousand times faster than the world's most powerful computer. A Petaflops computer is so far beyond anything within contemporary experience that its architecture, technology, and programming methods may prove radically different from anything envisioned today. To get a glimmer of this over-the-horizon future and prepare policy makers and research planners alike to lead the U.S. into the next century of hyper-computing, the first workshop on "Enabling Technologies for Petaflops Computing" was held on February 22–24, 1994 in Pasadena, California. Sponsored by six federal agencies, this workshop brought together more than 60 invited participants from industry, academia, and government who are experts in device technology, architecture, system software and tools, and applications and algorithms. Their goal was to produce the first comprehensive assessment of the technologies needed for Petaflops computing systems and to establish a baseline of understanding of its opportunities, challenges, and critical elements with the intent of setting near-term research directions.

This book attempts to establish a foundation of understanding as it captures the important findings and background details of the workshop. The intent of this foundation is to 1) enable technical policy makers to plan future research programs, 2) provide a framework of future advances in which researchers can position their own active work, and 3) fix a starting point from which future examinations of the needs of Petaflops computing can advance forward. In one sense, the success of the book will be determined by future near-term undertakings to explore further the far reaches of Petaflops computing. If such future investigations build on the findings and content of this book rather than repeating the same process, then it will be a success and will have made the contribution for which it was intended.

Enabling Technologies for Petaflops Computing reports the key findings of the workshop and their implications. An introductory chapter is followed by a description of the workshop methodology and transcripts of keynote addresses by Seymour Cray and Konstantin Likharev. Chapters 3–7 focus on the four working groups that examined devices, software, architecture, and applications. A chapter is dedicated to each group's findings, providing explanations for the group's conclusions. A short chapter summarizes the principal topics and results of each group. The remaining chapters look at the results of the workshop from a broad perspective, discussing their implications for future directions and identifying unresolved issues. Finally, the book gives recommendations drawn from the body of work to give explicit direction for follow-up studies. These recommendations, if pursued, will establish initial research paths toward realizing effective Petaflops computing systems sometime in the next two decades.

Acknowledgments

The authors of this book wish to thank all the workshop participants for making it a historical event in the evolution of high-performance computing. The four working group chairs: Carl Kukkonen, Harold Stone, Bert Halstead, and Geoffrey Fox are to be acknowledged for important leadership they provided throughout the process culminating with this book. In addition, the authors wish to acknowledge the important contributions made by several associates who were responsible for the excellent workshop arrangements and the high professional quality of this publication. Michael MacDonald provided technical editing, reviewing all aspects of this book and contributing substantively to a number of its sections. Terri Canzian provided exhaustive and detailed editing of the entire text and is responsible for the document's professional format and typesetting. Tina Pauna's painstaking editing weeded out countless awkward phrases and glitches. Tim Brice is credited for the success of the local arrangements and excellent logistical support throughout the workshop. Michele O'Connell provided important assistance to the workshop organizers prior to, during, and following the workshop and was responsible for coordination between the organizing committee, program committee, and local arrangements. Mary Goroff, Erla Solomon, and Chip Chapman assisted with registration, computers and copying equipment, and in handling the many details that arise in the course of a dynamic workshop. The editors are pleased to acknowledge the sponsorship of this workshop by NASA, NSF, DOE, ARPA, NSA, and BMDO. Finally, the editors convey their appreciation to MIT Press for its contribution in achieving the highest possible quality for the publication of this book.

Enabling Technologies for Petaflops Computing

1 Introduction

As the twentieth century draws to a close, it is becoming clear that prosperity and security in future decades will depend largely on productivity and efficiency in an increasingly competitive international market place. Crucial to leadership in the rapidly changing global economy are capabilities in developing, manufacturing, and applying high-performance computing and information management technologies. However, a combination of tightening constraints on the resources that can be dedicated to R&D and the accelerating pace of technical innovation have increased the complexity of setting research directions that will lead to major increases in capabilities for computing and information management. Such advances may take decades and will depend on much earlier work that creates the necessary enabling technologies and develops new capabilities in design and production. To create those strategic technologies it is necessary to begin planning efforts now to (1) establish long-term national technical goals, (2) identify enabling technologies for which near-term and long-term R&D are critical, (3) determine research agendas to meet these needs, and (4) prepare for support of initiatives in selected directions.

This book captures the findings of a historic meeting of key technical leaders and developers in high-performance computing that was convened to set the trajectory of technology investment and innovation over the next two decades to reach a target of sustainable Petaflops performance capability. A Petaflops is a million billion operations (or floating point operations) per second and is ten thousand times faster than what is achieved by today's fastest computers. No goal envisioned will be more challenging, demand greater advance planning, require more coordination and collaboration among all sectors of the high-performance computing community, or more strongly influence all facets of computing into the next century.

1.1 Overview

The Workshop on Enabling Technologies for Petaflops Computing was held on February 22 through 24, 1994. More than 60 experts in all facets of high-performance computing technology met to establish the basis for considering future research initiatives that will lead the development, production, and application of Petaflops scaled computing systems. In so doing, they considered diverse future technologies and assessed their potential. The objectives of the workshop were to identify applications requiring Petaflops performance and determine their resource demands; determine the scope of the technical challenge to achieving effective Petaflops computing; identify critical enabling technologies that can lead to Petaflops computing capability; establish key research issues; recommend elements of a near-term research agenda.

The workshop focused on four major and interrelated topic areas:
- Applications and Algorithms
- Device Technology
- Architecture
- Software Technology

Separate working groups were organized for each topic. Representatives from industry, academia, and government provided expertise in all four disciplines. The mix of talents and base of experience of this group across the spectrum of issues led to strong cross fertilization of ideas and interdisciplinary discussions which resulted in important findings.

The importance of this workshop to establishing long-term directions in high-performance computing systems research and development was emphasized by the strong sponsorship of many federal agencies. Each agency has a vested interest in U.S. capability in this field and considers it critical to carrying out its respective mission. The sponsoring agencies were:

- National Aeronautics and Space Agency
- National Science Foundation
- Department of Energy
- Advanced Research Projects Agency
- National Security Agency
- Ballistic Missile Defense Organization.

This book documents the issues addressed and the findings resulting from the three-day workshop. It is structured for use by both policy makers and researchers in setting goals and establishing programs to respond to the challenges of achieving Petaflops computing. In this book the reader will find the following: the complete reports of each of the working groups; summaries of the working group reports; the major findings of the workshop; analysis and discussion of the findings and their implications for the future of high-performance computing; recommendations and conclusions for near-term directions.

1.2 Objectives

The primary goal of this workshop was to conduct and disseminate the first comprehensive assessment of the field of Petaflops computing systems and to establish a baseline of understanding with respect to its opportunities, challenges, and critical elements at this, its inchoate phase. With a new understanding of this emerging field, a second guiding goal was to set near-term directions for further inquiry to refine the knowledge and reduce uncertainty in this field. With these goals established, the following set of objectives was identified and provided to guide the workshop agenda and deliberations:

Identify the Applications

Identify applications that require Petaflops performance that are and will be important to the economic, scientific, and societal well-being of the country. Determine resource requirements demanded by these problems at the specified scale.

Determine the Challenge

Determine the scope of the technical challenge to achieving Petaflops computing capability that is efficient, readily programmable, of general applicability, and economically viable. Relate these challenges to the current state of the art and identify near-term barriers toward progress in this direction.

Reveal the Enabling Technologies

Identify critical enabling technologies that lead to Petaflops computing capability. Consider alternative approaches and specify the pacing technologies that will determine the ultimate realization of this scale of computing system. For each alternative, indicate the pacing technologies that currently are not supported at a necessary sustaining level of funding.

Derive Research Issues

Establish key issues requiring further research. These issues should set the boundary between current state-of-the-art and the next regime intrinsic to achieving the four order-of-magnitude advance. These research issues should be the critical path ideas to the leading potential approaches.

Identify a Research Agenda

Recommend elements of a near-term research agenda. The proposed research topics should focus on immediate questions contributing to the uncertainty of understanding and imposing the greatest risk to launching a major long-term research initiative. Fulfilling such a short-term research program should allow planners and researchers to project a long-term research program toward Petaflops computing with confidence, and to justify the investment at the necessary level of funding.

1.3 Approach

The sponsoring agencies, the organizing committee, and the program committee convened the workshop to emphasize technical deliberations among a selected group of experts to consider the technical ramifications of the challenging goals set before them.

Four working groups were established with chair and co-chairs determined prior to the meeting. These were the

- Applications and Algorithms Working Group
  Chair – Geoffrey Fox (Syracuse University)
  Co-Chair – Rick Stevens (Argonne National Laboratory)
- Device Technology Working Group
  Chair – Carl Kukkonen (Jet Propulsion Laboratory)
  Co-Chair – John Neff (University of Colorado)
  Co-Chair – Doc Bedard (National Security Agency)
  Co-Chair – Joe Brewer (Westinghouse Electric Corporation)

- Architecture and Systems Working Group
  Chair – Harold Stone (IBM Corporation)
  Co-Chair – Thomas Sterling (USRA CESDIS)
- Software Technology Working Group
  Chair – Bert Halstead (Digital Equipment Corporation)
  Co-Chair – Bill Carlson (Supercomputing Research Center)

Each of the working groups was comprised of approximately a dozen experts from industry, academia, and government representing experience in the implementation, applications, and research of high-performance computing systems. The working groups were directed by the program committee to consider a number of questions as they related to the specific topic areas. The questions addressed were

1. What is the state of the art in your area?
2. What is the level of investment being made ($, work force, facilities)?
3. What is the current focus of advanced work?
4. Define key metrics of figures of merit that measure scale/capability in your area. In such terms, estimate the current rate of progress.
5. What are the barriers and challenges?
6. List the potential opportunities for significant advances that may overcome these major barriers and challenges. Include both evolutionary and revolutionary advances. Indicate primary intermediate accomplishments that would exemplify progress in those directions.
7. In chart form, relate figures of merit to intermediate accomplishments and estimate the most likely rate of progress against calendar years through the end of the decade.
8. What order-of-magnitude investment in funding, time, and human resources is required to achieve goals assuming favorable outcome of experimental work?

Not every question was germane to all the working group subjects. It was often difficult or impossible to give exact or complete responses in light of current knowledge. Nevertheless, these questions had a strong and positive influence on focusing the participants on issues that led to the important findings.

The workshop met in a series of plenary and working sessions. The first five questions were intended to force sharing of evolving thinking across working groups. The latter three were to provide the concentrated time for deep examination issues of the independent groups. Often, these split into splinter groups to work separately on specific core or critical path issues.

Prior to the workshop each working group formulated its respective position on the state of the art in its field and the key problems as currently perceived. At the first plenary session, the chairs of each working group presented these position statements to the entire workshop to establish a shared context. Also, at the inaugural meeting Seymour Cray and Konstantin Likharev each gave a presentation to set the tone of the workshop and to initiate the debate that was to continue for the remaining three days.

At the conclusion of the workshop, each working group presented its closing positions and identified questions left unresolved. Contributors worked together to write the final report for each working group. Also, the program committee worked to identify cross-cut issues and findings and to synthesize them into a single coherent structure.

1.4 Background

The goal of achieving sustained Teraflops computing by the end of the decade is the focus of the Federal HPCC program. While many challenges to realizing efficient and cost-effective systems and techniques still exist, the general approach has been prescribed. For example, it is clear that in this time frame, ensembles of between 1,000 to 10,000 superscalar microprocessors will be implemented to deliver peak performance at the Teraflops scale. Software methodologies to support massively parallel processing systems are still in advanced development, but general approaches are well founded. The high-performance computing (HPC) community can anticipate that, given continued investment in the necessary R&D, the HPCC program will achieve its performance goals in the allotted time.

Given the progress of the HPCC program toward its goal, it is time for industry, academia, and government to begin addressing the more daunting challenge of positioning future long-term research programs to develop enabling technologies for Petaflops computing systems. The HPCC program was enacted to confirm U.S. competitiveness in the world's high technology market place; to sustain preeminence will demand that the U.S. HPC community move aggressively beyond the Teraflops milestone to tackle the staggering goal of realizing and harnessing Petaflops capability.

The achievement of Gigaflops performance demanded a paradigm shift from previous conventional computing methods in architecture, technology, and software. Vector processing, integrated high-speed devices, vectorizing languages and compilers, and dense packaging techniques were incorporated into a single supercomputer model culminating in such a tour de force as the CRAY C-90. Similarly, the achievement of Teraflops performance, which the community is actively pursuing, is demanding a second paradigm shift exploiting VLSI technology, massively parallel processing architectures, as well as messaging-passing and data-parallel programming models. The first of these advances (vector processing) was a product of industrial development with government-sponsored research in applications and software technology. The second of these advances, scalable parallel computing, is requiring a much larger cooperative initiative harnessing the capabilities and talents of all elements of the HPC community. The first advance occurred largely spontaneously through the creativity and initiative of the industrial and user community; the second required years of prior planning involving joint federal agency coordination, as well as broad community involvement and support.

Drawing upon this history to anticipate the nature of the challenge imposed by goals of effective Petaflops computation, it can be assumed that the next revolutionary step from Teraflops to Petaflops capability will be achieved only through yet another multifaceted paradigm shift in architecture, technology, and software methods. Concepts and capabilities not usually associated with mainline HPC community may prove key to the new paradigm. Further, the cooperation and integration of our national resources, even beyond that exemplified throughout the HPCC program, will be critical to success. Coordination and direction of research toward these goals will require substantial planning drawing upon expertise and insights of professionals from all parts of the high-performance computing community. Even as the HPCC program is underway, initial planning for the next step must be undertaken so that upon successful conclusion of the HPCC program the government will be prepared to maintain the momentum and redirect it toward the follow-on goals.

Early recognition of the importance of this issue has come from the NASA Administrator. At his request in 1992, a panel was convened to consider the domain of issues expected to impact significantly progress toward Petaflops computing systems. A Supercomputing Special Initiative Team comprising key personnel from NASA Headquarters and HPCC centers was formed to "evaluate whether the U.S. high-performance computing community is aggressively supporting NASA's existing and future computing requirements," with the objective of recommending, "program or policy changes to better support NASA's [high-performance computing] interests." The team explored NASA HPC requirements over the next decade, examined current government-supported efforts in HPC, evaluated efforts by the U.S. supercomputing industry and those overseas, and formulated recommendations to the NASA Administrator.

NASA concluded that its mission requirements will demand Petaflops capability, but that there are major barriers to achieving it. The team also observed that NASA alone could not exert sufficient influence on developments in many of the areas that may contribute to the elimination of these barriers. The team recommended that NASA join with other agencies to sponsor architectural studies of Petaflops computing systems. Cooperation of this type would ensure that mission requirements of all federal agencies affect the priorities of technology development initiatives toward a Petaflops capability.

It was determined that, in cooperation with other agencies, NASA should sponsor a focused in-depth workshop on enabling technologies for Petaflops computing. The purpose of such a workshop would be to determine research directions critical to achieving a Petaflops capability. While this general topic has been considered in other forums such as the Purdue Workshop on Grand Challenges in Computer Architecture for Support of High Performance Computing in 1991, it has not been addressed from a perspective that includes federal agency mission requirements, nor from a view to initiating near-term research programs. Results from the Purdue workshop and various conference panels were first steps in this direction but have not yielded sufficient detailed findings to provide specific research direction. It is important to note that with Teraflops capability still a scientific and engineering challenge, there was a danger of a Petaflops workshop appearing superfluous to the community. Therefore, it would be crucial that objectives and methodology be well defined so that the workshop could garner the respect of the NASA and HPC communities by providing the first detailed examination of the issues relevant to achieving Petaflops computing.

In determining the scope of the challenge, the workshop was to delineate clearly the limitations of conventional and expected near-term approaches to implementing and applying Petaflops-scale systems. A number of exotic technologies, architectures, and methodologies have been pursued in academia and industry. These laboratory explorations were to be examined for their potential in achieving Petaflops capability. The most promising avenues of pursuit should be characterized in terms of the pivotal technical issues that restrain their advance, i.e., the dominant research questions in the field. Having identified these research issues, the workshop would formulate a long-term approach to research in Petaflops computing, including alternative paths to be considered and their interplay with world-wide integrated information and computing resources. Finally, the workshop would deliver specific and detailed recommendations for new research initiatives aimed at reducing the uncertainty in this field.

1.5 Technical Challenges

While a myriad of issues present themselves as relevant to the broad question of Petaflops computing systems, four major areas were identified as having been of critical importance to past generational changes in high-performance computing. These areas are

- Device Technology
- System Architecture
- Programming Models and Software Technology
- Applications and Algorithms.

Device technology determines the maximum clock rate of a computing system and the density of its component packaging. Semiconductor technology has provided the basis for many of the important advances over the preceding two decades, but important alternatives are being investigated that may enable significant performance advances. Among these alternatives are optical devices and superconducting devices. Optical devices provide alternative approaches to communications, storage, and processing with important advantages over their semiconductor counterparts in each case. Superconducting devices have been explored as a basis for computing systems for over a decade and have been shown to yield substantial performance advantage compared to conventional semiconductor devices. Other exotic technologies may also merit consideration. Beyond the device material physics, the form of the basic computing elements may be subject to change. The conventional use of Boolean gates may need rethinking. Hybrids of digital and analog processing devices may provide significant potential for speedup. Technologies that permit much denser packing or higher interconnectivity, such as those proposed for neural nets, might enable a scale of parallelism unprecedented in today's system framework.

While useful for establishing a baseline, the approach of harnessing off-the-shelf workstation processors in large, highly-interconnected ensembles is unlikely to move the performance curve to Petaflops levels. The issues of latency, overhead, and load balancing that are already proving to be major challenges in achieving Teraflops-scale computing with MPPs will dominate systems where the speed-of-light distance of one clock cycle will be a fraction of a Wafer Scale Integration (WSI) die. The underlying model of computation reflected by both the system architecture and the programming model may involve serious alteration or even replacement as ease-of-use issues for managing these highly complex systems dominate effectiveness. Much functionality currently found in software will migrate to hardware as runtime information becomes critical for optimizing scheduling and data migration. Assuming that parallelism exploitation will be key to success of Petaflops execution, management of fine-grain tasks and synchronization will further encourage hardware realization of new support mechanisms. Many advanced concepts in parallel architecture have been studied but have failed to compete on an economic basis with conventional incremental advances. A close examination of the underlying concepts of the best of these architecture models will reveal new directions that may dominate system structures for Petaflops class platforms.

The early experience with massively parallel processing is revealing the importance of the interface between the user and the high-performance computing system on which the application is performed. Many difficulties are being encountered that show the need for improved tools to assist in achieving program correctness and performance optimization. Much of the difficulty results from the incremental approach programmers have taken from uniprocessor programming methodologies to parallel programming techniques. Message-passing methods are yielding only slowly to data-parallel programming techniques and these are not likely in and of themselves to fully satisfy the needs of all major scientific and engineering problems. Fundamental problems still exist in this highly complex relationship and these must be highlighted. Research in alternative methods has been pursued but little of it has found its way into day-to-day scientific computing. However, these advanced concepts may prove essential for organizing computation on systems logically ten-thousand times larger than today's most substantial systems. Object-oriented, message-driven, and functional programming models may be required in a single framework to manage complexity and master scalable correctness.

Petaflops computing systems are only justified if problems of major importance can be identified requiring such capabilities. Even as the HPCC program works toward the goal of usable Teraflops, it is becoming apparent that many problems of engineering and scientific importance will require performance and storage capacity in excess of that anticipated for the Teraflops machines. In speculating on such problems, the balance of resources as they scale through four orders of magnitude must be understood for real problems. Simply scaling each system parameter by a factor of 10,000 may not be appropriate for the applications that require Petaflops computers. For example, for some problems communication requirements can be anticipated to scale nonlinearly for interprocessor and I/O needs, but the degree of change is poorly understood. Is it possible that a Petaflops system will be largely an I/O hub? Or, will interprocessor communication be the dominant resource investment instead of memory? Without direction from application program scaling evaluation, the entire organization of Petaflops computer systems will be in doubt.

By focusing device technology, architectures, applications, and software technology, the workshop sought to provide the basis for understanding the challenges, opportunities, and approaches to achieving and effectively using Petaflops performance. These areas are not orthogonal to each other, but rather are mutually supportive. Each contributes to the context of the others. Each provides constraints on the others. And each may supply some of the solutions to problems presented by the others. It was the task of the workshop to untangle these relationships in the regime of Petaflops operation and establish new directions that reflect the insights gained from such an evaluation.

2. Petaflops from Two Perspectives

2.1 Seymour Cray Keynote Address

The following text is an invited talk given at Petaflops Workshop Pasadena, CA, January 1994.

Seymour Cray
Cray Computer Corporation

I understand we could characterize our group today as a constructive lunatic fringe group. I would like to start off presenting what I think is today's reality, but then I'll move into the lunatic area a little later. I would like to give you three impressions today. The first one is my view of where we are today in terms of scientific computer technology. The second one is, what's the rate of progress that we, Cray Computer Corporation, are making incrementally? By incrementally I mean in a few years. And thirdly, I'd like to speculate on what I would do if I were going to take a really radical approach to a revolutionary step such as we are talking about in this workshop.

What I want to do is talk about the things I know myself, and I think we are representative of where other companies are as well. In order to have some real numbers to be specific, I'll talk about my own work for a few minutes. The CRAY 4 computer is a current effort and we should complete the machine this year. We should look at the number of Gigaflops—and this is where I'd like to start—and at what they cost in today's prices. I would like to separate the memory issue for just a moment from the processors because they are somewhat different. If I do that, then the cost per Gigaflops in a CRAY 4 is $80,000. Now, I look at the incremental progress and project it four years, and I use four years because that's the kind of step we do in building machines: two years is too fast, but four years is about right. So if I use four years as my increment of time, and I ask what do we expect to do in that time, this gives us a rate of change. I see a factor of four every four years and I have every reason to believe that in the next four years we can continue at that rate. Whether we can continue at that rate forever, I don't know, but it is a rate that has some history and some credibility.

If I look forward four years, we are going to have a conventional vector machine with about $20,000 per Gigaflops, for the processor.

What does it cost per Teraflops? We are talking $20,000,000. Now we have to add memory. One of the rules of thumb we have in vector processing is for every Gigaflops in processor you need a Gigaword per second bandwidth to a common memory, and this makes the memory expensive. It's the bandwidth more than memory size that actually determines the cost. The memory cost varies somewhat from a minimum of about the cost of the processors to twice the cost of the processors. So if I pick a number, in between or 1 1/2 times that for a very big system, we would find we would have a Teraflops conventional vector machine in four years for around $50,000,000. I think that's reality without any special effort apart from normal competition in the business.

I'd like to look at the other end of the spectrum because I have been involved in that recently. By the other end of the spectrum, I mean a step from a cost of $80,000 or $20,000 per processor to the other extreme end, about $6 per processor. That, in fact, is another machine we are building at Cray Computer. If we look at SIMD bit-processing, that is the other end of the spectrum, so to speak. Of course, the purpose of building this is not to do Gigaflops, Teraflops, or Petaflops but to do image processing, but never mind that for a moment. I want to come up with a cost figure here. What we are building is a 2,000,000-processor SIMD machine and it will cost around $12,000,000 to build. We are planning to make a 32,000,000-processor system in four years, and that will have a Peta-operation per second. My point is, if you program bit processors to do floating point, which may not be the most efficient thing in the world, you still come up with a machine that can do around Teraflops in four years. Whether you take a very large processor or a very small processor, either way we come up with about a Teraflops and about $50,000,000 in four years. I suspect, although I don't really know, that if we try various kinds of processor speeds in between, we're going be somewhere in the same ballpark. So my conclusion is that in four years we could have a Teraflops and it ought to cost about $50,000,000 and the price ought to drop pretty fast thereafter.

So, how do we get another factor of a thousand? Well if we are able to maintain our current incremental rate, it will take 20 years. Now that might be too slow I don't know what our goals are in this exercise. I suspect it might take 20 years anyway, but if we'd like to have both belt and suspenders, we could try a revolutionary approach and so I have a favorite one that I would like to propose. It's probably different from everyone else's.

I think in order to get to a Petaflops within a reasonable period of time, or 10 years, we have to somehow reduce the size of our components (see, I am really a device person) from the micron size to the nanometer size. I don't think we can really build a machine that fills room after room after room and costs an equivalent numbers of dollars. We have to make something roughly the size of present machines, but with a thousand times the components. And, if I understand my physics right, that means we need to be in the nanometer range instead of the micrometer range. Well, that's hard, but there are a lot of exciting things happening in the nanometer-size range right now. During the past year, I have read a number of articles that make my jaw drop. They aren't from our community. They are from the molecular biology community, and I can imagine two ways of riding the coat tails of a much bigger revolution than we have. One way would be to attempt to make computing elements out of biological devices. Now, I'm not very comfortable with that because I am one and I feel threatened. I prefer the second course, which is to use biological devices to manufacture non-biological devices: to manufacture only the things that are more familiar to us and are more stable, in the sense that we understand them better. What evidence do we have that this is possible? Two areas really have impressed me, again, almost all during the past year. The rates of understanding in the nanometer world are just astounding. I don't know how many of you are following this area, but I have been attempting to read abstracts of papers, and some of them are just mind-boggling. Let me just digress for a moment with the understanding of the nanometer world as I perceive it with my superficial knowledge from reading abstracts.

First, I once thought of a cell as sort of a chemical engineer's creation. It was a bag filled with fluid, mostly water, with proteins floating around inside doing goodness knows what. Well, my perception in the past year has certainly changed because I understand now they're not full of water at all. And if we look inside, as we are beginning to do with tools that are equally mind-boggling, we see that we have a whole lot of protein factories scattered around, hundreds and thousands of them in a single cell, with a smaller number of power plants scattered around, and a transportation system that interconnects all of these things with railroad tracks. Now, in case any of you think I'm on drugs, I brought some documentation. You can read these government-sponsored reports, which you have to believe are real, because it's our tax dollars that pay for this. But I'm coming to the part that's most interesting to me. Using laser tweezers, which has been the big breakthrough in seeing what's going on in the nanometer world, human researchers have been able to take a section of the railroad track of the cell, put it on a glass slide, and lo and behold there's a train running on it with a locomotive and four cars. We can measure the speed and we did. The track is not smooth. It has indents in it every 8 nanometers. It's a cog railroad. When we measure the locomotive speed, we see it isn't smooth. The locomotive moves in little 8 nanometer jerks. When it does, it burns one unit of power from the power plant, which is an ATP molecule. So it burns one molecule and it moves one step. Well, how fast does it do this? It does it every few milliseconds. In other words, the locomotive moves many times its own length in a second. This is a fast locomotive. I am obviously impressed with the mechanical nature of what we are learning about in the large molecule world.

What evidence is there that we could get anything to make a non-biological device? Or, to come right to the point, how do we train bacteria to make transistors? Well I don't know how to do that right now, but last spring there was a very interesting experiment in cell replicating of copper wire. It's a nano-tube built with a whole row of copper atoms. The purpose of the experiment was not to make a computer, it was to penetrate the wall of the cell and measure their potentials inside without upsetting the cell's activity. These people are in a different area of concern here. But, if indeed we can make copper wire that grows itself, and this copper wire was three nanometers in diameter insulated and if we can do that today, isn't it conceivable that we can create bacteria that make something more complicated tomorrow?

So, what course of action might we take to explore nanometer devices that are self-replicating. It seems to me we have to have some cross-fertilization among government agencies here. There are people doing very worthwhile research in the sense of finding the causes and cures for diseases, and more power to them, keep going. But maybe we can fund some research more directed toward making non-biological devices using the same nanometer mechanisms. So, that's my radical proposal for how we might proceed. I don't really know what kind of cross-fertilization we can get in this area, or whether any of you think this is a worthwhile idea, but it's going to be interesting for me to hear your proposals on how we get a factor of a thousand in a quick period and this is just one idea. I thank you and am ready to hear your ideas.

2.2 Konstantin Likharev Keynote Address

Invited talk given at Petaflops Workshop Pasadena, CA, January 1994

SUPERFAST COMPUTATION USING SUPERCONDUCTOR CIRCUITS
Konstantin K. Likharev
State University of New York, Stony Brook, NY

I am grateful to the organizers of this very interesting meeting for inviting me here to speak at this plenary session. I am happy to do that, mostly because I honestly believe that what is happening right now in digital superconductor electronics is a real revolution which deserves the attention of a wide audience. Before I start I should mention my major collaborators at SUNY (M. Bhushan, P. Bunyk, J. Lin, J. Lukens, A. Oliva, S. Polonsky, D. Schneider, P. Shevchenko, V. Semenov, and D. Zinoviev), as well as the organizations with which we are collaborating (HYPRES, IBM, NIST, Tektronix, and Westinghouse), and also the support of our work at SUNY by DoD's University Research Initiative, IBM, and Tektronix. I should also draw your attention to a couple of available reviews of this field [Likharev:93a,94a].

Arnold Silver, who in fact was one of the founding fathers of the field, already gave you some of its flavor, but I believe I should nevertheless repeat some key points. As Table 2.1 shows, superconductor integrated circuits offer several unparalleled advantages over semiconductor transistor circuits. (There are serious problems, too, but I will discuss them later). The advantages, surprisingly enough, start not with active elements. As Steven Pei mentioned earlier today, the real speed of semiconductor VLSI circuits has almost nothing to do with the speed of the transistors employed. It is limited mostly by charging of capacitances of interconnects through output resistances of the transistors. Superconductors have the unique capability to transfer signals (including picosecond waveforms) not in a diffusive way like the RC-type charging, but ballistically with a speed approaching that of light. (When you listen

Table 2.1
Superconductor Digital Circuits

Superconducting Transmission Lines
— ballistic transfer of picosecond waveforms
— small crosstalk

Josephson Junctions
— picosecond waveform generation
— impedance matching to transmission lines
— low dissipation $\frac{(\Rightarrow \text{high density})}{(\Rightarrow \text{high speed})}$

Fabrication Technology
— very simple (low-T_c)

---

to a talk on opto-electronics like the one earlier today, always remember that it is not necessary to have light if what you need is just the speed of light.) In order to achieve the ballistic transfer in superconductors, it is sufficient to use a simple passive microstrip transmission line, with the thin film strip a few tenths of a micron over a superconducting ground plane. Because of this small distance, the electromagnetic field is well localized within the gap, so that the crosstalk between neighboring transmission lines, parallel or crossing, is very small.

In order to generate picosecond waveforms, we need appropriate generators, and for that Josephson junctions (weak contacts between superconductors) are very convenient. One other good thing about the Josephson junctions is that their impedance can be matched with that of the microstrip lines. This means that the picosecond signal can be in fact injected into the transmission line for ballistic propagation. Finally, superconductor circuits work with very small signals, typically of the order of one millivolt. Therefore, even with the impedance matching, the power dissipation remains low (I will show you some figures later on). Because of this small power dissipation, you can pack devices very close to each other on a chip, and locate chips very close together. This factor again reduces the propagation delays, and increases speed.

Finally, one more advantage: superconductor fabrication technology is extremely simple (if we are speaking about low-T_c superconductors). It is considerably simpler than silicon CMOS technology and much simpler than the gallium arsenide technologies. At SUNY, we are fabricating superconductor integrated circuits. With our facilities we would certainly not be able to run, say, a CMOS process. From "semiconductor peoples" point of view, all we are doing is simply several levels of metallization on the intact silicon substrate. Typically, there are three to four layers of niobium, one layer of a resistive film, and two to three layers of insulation (Josephson junctions are formed by thin aluminum oxide barriers between two niobium films). Several niobium foundries in this country are available to fabricate such circuits for you.

What has been going on in this field and what is going on now? You probably have heard about the large-scale IBM project and the Japanese project, with a goal to develop a superfast computer using Josephson junctions. Unfortunately, both projects were based on the so-called latching circuits where two DC voltage levels, low and high, were used to present binary information, just as in semiconductors. The left column of Table 2.2 lists major features of the latching circuits. Unfortunately, their maximum clock frequency was only slightly higher than 1 GHz, and theoretical estimates show that it can hardly go higher than about 3 GHz. In my view, this is too slow to compete with semiconductors, because you should compensate the necessity of low-temperature operation.

Is there any other opportunity? Yes, there is one. In superconductors, there is one basic property that we can use for computing. Namely, the magnetic flux through any superconducting loop is quantized: it can only equal an integer number of the fundamental unit $\Phi_0 = h/2e$. Of course it is natural to use this number for coding digital data. Thus, any superconductor ring is quite sufficient for the storage of digital information. But for switching, e.g., for writing the information in or reading it out, we need some device for the rapid transfer of the flux in or out of the loop. In our circuits, we do it by inserting a weak link, the Josephson junction, into the loop. When one flux quantum Φ_0 enters or leaves the loop, a picosecond pulse with the area

$$V(t)dt = \Phi_0^2 mV - ps \qquad (2.2.1)$$

Table 2.2

	Latching Circuits	RSFQ Circuits
Data Presentation	voltage	Magnetic Flux
Natural Quantization	no	yes ($\Phi_0 = h/2e$)
Power Consumption	~ 3 pcW/gate	~ 0.3 pcW/gate
Power Supply	AC	DC
SC Wiring Layer	3	2
Self-time Possible	no	yes
Maximum Speed	~ 3 GHz	~ 300 GHz

is generated across the junction according to Faraday's law. This "Single-Flux-Quantum" (SFQ) pulse can, in turn, be used to switch other similar circuits. Thus, if you abandon information coding by voltage levels, but use magnetic flux for this purpose, you can do everything very fast.

The right column in Table 2.2 shows you what we can do using such an approach. We call it RSFQ, which stands for Rapid Single-Flux-Quantum circuits. I believe this table is self-explanatory. We use magnetic flux. Power consumption goes down. But of course you should concentrate on the last line showing speed. It is not pure theory. This figure (300 GHz) comes from experiments, complemented by a little bit of extrapolation to slightly better design rules.

We suggested the RSFQ approach as a whole in 1985. Of course, it was based on a lot of previous work, in particular on some of our preliminary work in the mid-70s, some ideas of Arnold Silver and his group (then at the Aerospace Corporation) in the late 1970s, and some Japanese ideas (especially from the Tohoku University group). But the real development of the RSFQ circuits started only in 1985, and only since 1991 has been going really fast. I do not have enough time to show you all the developed circuitry, so that I will just give you an idea of how these circuits are working.

In the simple circuits for generation of the SFQ pulses in which we are using Josephson junctions, information coded in the usual way (by voltage/current levels) arrives at its input, and an SFQ pulse is generated at its output. A simple logic gate, the invertor, uses just three Josephson junctions. How complex are other gates? Sometimes a little bit more complex than those in silicon, sometimes a little bit simpler, but always comparable in terms of, say, Josephson junction count in comparison with $p - n$ junction count in CMOS. We have designed another gate which is a sort of template—a universal gate, potentially with four inputs and six outputs. A slight modification (typically, a truncation) of this template can give you virtually any basic logic function.

Finally, when you have all your logic done in the form of the magnetic flux (or, equivalently, the picosecond SFQ pulses), and you feel you are tired of this superfast processing, you can always transform these SFQ pulses to DC voltage level output. This voltage can be picked up by a normal amplifier. We have demonstrated an extremely simple single-bit interface between RSFQ circuits and room-temperature semiconductor electronics at a data rate slightly below one Gigabit per second, with the parts costing less than $20 per channel.

Now, what is the current state of the fabrication technology? Though the circuit complexity is still not very exciting, the speed is. For example, consider a very simple digital circuit that we have designed, just a frequency divider by two (in other words, a single stage of a binary counter) which is modification of a device which was first conceived by Arnold Silver. We have implemented it using 1.2-micron, $8\,\text{kA}/\text{cm}^2$ niobium technology. It is fabricated in the usual university lab for not very much money, and we have made measurements that prove that this circuit can divide the frequency of the input SFQ pulse train, for any frequency from 0 to 510 GHz. To be honest, it is not a completely digital device. If you fabricated a regular logic gate, say, with two inputs and two outputs, using this particular technology, the maximum speed would be around 100 GHz.

We are still not doing so well in the terms of complexity, because we started our program at SUNY just two years ago. The most complex circuit which we are testing right now (it was developed by us, but fabricated by HYPRES, Inc.) has 645 Josephson junctions and about 1,000 resistors. Clearly, this is still not very large-scale integration. We

Table 2.3
32 × 32-bit multipliers based on various digital circuit technologies

Circuit Type: Fabrication Technology	Design Rules (μm)	Integration Scale (10^3 Josephson or $p-n$ junctions)	Throughput (10^9 Operations per second)	Latency (ns)
parallel-pipelined; SC-MOS	1.0	200	0.2	150
parallel; JJ latching	1.0	70	1.5	1
Serial; JJ RSFQ	1.0	1.5	1.5	1
Parallel-pipelined JJ RSFQ	1.0	40	100	1

have, however, an ambitious two-year plan. Each year we are going to increase the integration scale by a factor of 10.

Now let me just summarize what we have. Table 2.3 shows the performance you can get at a typical computation task, multiplication of two 32-bit operands as fast as possible. If you do it in the silicon technology with one micron minimum feature size, you would need about 100,000 transistors to do the job (in a bit-parallel-pipelined structure to provide the maximum speed). You would get a not very spectacular latency, but relatively high throughput. If you do the same task using the old (latching) Josephson logic, you could have approximately the same circuit complexity, and do it about seven times faster. I don't believe this advantage is very big. But with this new superconductor electronics (RSFQ) you can, for one thing, accomplish the task with approximately the same speed (several times faster than silicon) by an extremely simple bit-serial circuit. This circuit, comprising only 1,500 Josephson junctions, will crunch the numbers bit by bit with this enormous clock frequency which is available on chip. This is the circuit complexity that we may achieve as soon as later this year. Alternatively, you could use the same RSFQ technology to do the same computation with all the bits processed in parallel. That would mean that the complexity of the chip would be much higher, almost the same as in silicon, but look at this throughput (100 Gigaflops for a single processor)! In comparison with silicon, I believe, we have at least 2.5 orders of magnitude advantage in speed.

The simple table (Table 2.4), which I have prepared for this workshop, may be even more interesting. Right now when we are using a niobium foundry with a relatively old 3-mm technology for circuit fabrication, we can do calculations at clock frequency of about 30 GHz (which would give us almost 30 Gigaflops if we do them in parallel), with very low power (3×10^{-2} Watt per processor). Now we at SUNY are in transition to our new 1.25-mm technology, where we hopefully will eventually be able to have about 100 Gigaflops per processor, with power consumption about 0.1 Watts. Finally, when eventually we use, for example, a 0.35-mm process (it will already be a rather complex technology, certainly not of the university caliber, but not much more complex than what the silicon people are doing right now), we would approach the natural limitation of speed of niobium RSFQ circuits at the level 300 GHz. Then the power dissipation would be close to the maximum which you can afford in liquid helium. (Unfortunately, at 4.2 K you cannot remove 30 Watts of power from a square centimeter of the chip surface, as you do routinely at 300 K. If you do nothing special, just put your chip into liquid helium, you can generate only about 0.3 Watts without substantial overheating. Probably better helium cooling systems could be developed, but nobody has worked on that problem much, to my knowledge).

Now, even if we concentrate at the second (1-mm) level of the technology, rather simple from the point of view of the silicon people, we are talking about something like 100 Gigaflops per processor. Hence, you would need only some 10,000 processors to reach 1 Petaflops. The total dissipated power would be about 1 kilowatt. Of course, memory would add something to this estimate. But remember that simple storage of information in this technology does not require power; dissipation is

Table 2.4
RSFQ: Expected Performance for a Petaflops Machine (@1 μm) $\sim 10^4$ processors $\times 0.1$ W each $\cong$ 1 kW

	Technology	Speed, GHz per Gflops	Power per Processor
Old	(3 μm)	30	3×10^{-2}
New	(1 μm)	100	10^{-1}
Prospective	(0.35 μm)	300	3×10^{-1}

only involved in read/write operations. So I do not believe that memory would add much to our estimate—probably a factor of two or three.

Of course, you should remember that this (1 kW) is the figure for dissipation in liquid helium. If you are speaking about the total power consumption at room temperature, you should multiply this number by at least 300. Fortunately, there is another factor. Of that 1 kilowatt I have mentioned only some 10 Watts would be dissipated in your Josephson junctions. Right now we use very conservative circuits which are, crudely speaking, some analog of n-MOS circuits in the silicon technology. In these circuits, most power dissipation takes place in resistors which do not really play any useful role. We are starting to work on a sort of complementary logic (which should be an analog of CMOS), and I hope we will be able to reduce this 1 kW to about 30 Watts at 4.2 K, which means that 1 Petaflops will cost us some 10 kW at 300 K, incomparably less than silicon or any other technology.

Do we have problems? Yes, we certainly do. But as you can see in Table 2.5, all our problems bear the dollar sign. The first problem is refrigeration. Even if you are using a single superconductor chip, a present-day closed-cycle cryocooler would cost about 10–20 thousand dollars. Of course, with introduction to mass applications this figure would go down, but nevertheless cooling with liquid helium always make the simple superconductor circuits more expensive than silicon. This is why I don't believe that this technology would ever be in PCs or even

Table 2.5
Major Problems of the RFSQ Technology

> 1. Helium Refrigeration (~$10–20 K/unit)
> 2. Large Memories (development $$)
> 3. Psychology ("$60 M problem")

workstations. It's something to be reserved for the high-performance end of computing.

Next, as far as we know, nothing in this technology prevents big memories. The limitations are essentially the same as in semiconductors. We are presently testing the first RSFQ memory cell, with an area of only 100 lithographic squares (i.e., smaller than semiconductor SRAM cells, though slightly larger than DRAM cells). Of course, to develop a real memory, you would need financial investment much larger than the one we are using now for the development of basic logic circuitry.

Finally, I believe there is what you would call a $60,000,000.00 problem of psychology. People are just not accustomed to these ideas. They are not accustomed to the idea of cooling or to other issues of superfast computation. For example, our circuits can use what is called the local self-timing, in particular, the hand-shaking protocol on the single-bit level. It means that you can use a flexible combination of synchronous and asynchronous computation. The asynchronous computation scares some people to death. This and many other issues should be not only explored, but also implanted into minds of electronic engineers.

Now, let me show you the last transparency (Table 2.6). It is a favorable scenario of the future development in this field. We see several small-scale market niches where I believe this technology would win, because we are far ahead of any competition in performance, and there are people around willing to pay money for that. One example is the famous SQUIDs, which are supersensitive magnetometers. People are using liquid helium to work with these devices now, so they certainly would be willing to do that when we improve the devices radically using some on-chip digital processing. Somewhere below the fourth line of this table I become much less confident. First of all, we should still

Table 2.6
RSFQ Technology: Forthcoming Applications (Favorable Scenario)

---

1. A/D Converters
   16 bits @ ~ 100 MHz $\sim 1,000$ JJ   1993–94

2. Digital SQUIDS
   10 fT/Hz$^{1/2}$ @ $\sim 10^{10} \frac{\Phi_0}{\text{Hz}}$ $\sim 1,500$ JJ   1994–95

3. Digital DC voltmeters and potentiometers
   30 bits @ 0.15 & 10 V $\sim 10,000$ JJ   1994–95

4. Digital signal processors @ intelligent switches
   ~ 3 Gflops/proc @ 32 bits $\sim 12,000$ JJ   1995–96

5. Dedicated Coprocessors for Supercomputing
   ??   1996–??

---

solve a lot of technical problems. Moreover, somewhere at this point we may come to the situation where we will need much stronger collaboration with architecture people, with potential users, and we will certainly need a much larger investment than we have right now if we want this revolution to continue all the way down to the Petaflops future.

3 Summary of Working Group Reports

This chapter presents a brief overview of the following four chapters and their findings. It is offered to facilitate gaining a global perspective of the many complex and interrelated issues prior to examining the individual reports in more depth. In so doing, it provides a guide to the remaining chapters of this part of the book.

3.1 Applications

A driving motivation for pursuing Petaflops capability is the wealth of applications that impose computing demands at that scale and that are of potential importance to our Nation's future economic, societal, and security needs. The Applications Working Group considered two important factors related to the realization and use of Petaflops computing systems: the class of problems that would make use of such capability, and the characteristics of the application demands on the computing resources. It was found that there were many such applications spanning a wide array of domains. These fell into the categories of large-scale simulations, data-intensive applications, and novel applications. A distinction among simulation problems for Petaflops computing is those whose problem size can grow to fill system capacity and those problems of fixed size requiring greatly extended simulated time. Data-intensive applications require storage capacity equaling or exceeding a Petabyte even when Petaflops performance may not be critical. Novel applications are those not yet identified but which can be anticipated to open entirely new forms of services for humanity with the advent and availability of Petaflops computers.

A number of applications that would benefit from availability of Petaflops performance were identified in each of the following major areas:

- biomedicine, biology, biochemistry
- chemistry, chemical engineering
- physics
- space science and astronomy
- artificial intelligence
- study of climate and weather
- environmental studies, monitoring, and prediction
- geophysics and petroleum engineering

- aerospace, mechanical, and manufacturing engineering
- military applications
- business operations.

These establish a firm basis of justification for Petaflops machines. The need for such computing capacity derives either from the physical structure of the problem or from the size of the large datasets. While all critical applications in the ensuing decades cannot be predicted, it can be anticipated that they will include extensions of problems from the areas mentioned above. It is expected that many such applications will take on an increasingly multidisciplinary character incorporating models of distinct but interacting regimes. Also, future applications will commit significant resources to advanced methods of user interface including scientific visualization and virtual reality which will be enabled by the availability of Petaflops capable systems.

A number of key characteristics of applications as they relate to architectures were identified. Among those, the following were particularly germane: requirements for Petaflops performance; need for new algorithms; problem size scaling characteristics with respect to performance; memory requirements; I/O requirements; mass storage requirements; locality and latency sensitivity; operating system support requirements; special user interface issues.

Among these, the question of required system memory capacity was among the most urgent because it fixed the time scale in which such architectures would become commercially viable. With the Architecture Working Group, it was determined that, for a wide range of simulation class applications, memory requirements scale less than linearly with performance such that a Petaflops system is likely to need no more than about 30 Terabytes of main memory, and probably less. This is not to say that there will not be problems that will make use of a Petabyte of memory. In some cases, such problems might not even need the full Petaflops performance capability but rather are memory intensive in nature. A detailed examination of a number of applications was conducted and the results of each case captured in Section 4.4 of this book.

In all likelihood, algorithms will have to evolve to make use of the unprecedented scale of performance, parallelism, and latency that the use of Petaflops machines will encompass. The scalability of today's problems to those at the Petaflops level will require advances in the serial complexity of the algorithm (algorithmic efficiency) and the parallelization efficiency. These requirements are often in conflict. It is anticipated that the hierarchical structure of Petaflops systems' memory and processor organization will favor algorithms that exhibit hierarchical abstract structure for synchronization and communication. But hierarchical algorithms are difficult to implement with perfect parallel efficiency. This challenge is compounded by issues of problem size scaling which do not always return comparable parallelism for increased problem size. Finally, precision of calculations may need to be increased as problem size grows. All of these issues require further study before our understanding of the impact on applications of Petaflops computing is definitive.

3.2 Device Technology

More than any other single domain, device technology establishes the opportunities and limitations imposed on the high-performance system developer. The history of computer architecture is to a significant degree a sequence of enhancements to instruction set and component organization architectures in response to advances in device technologies. In preparing the possible paths toward Petaflops system structures, it is essential to anticipate future trends and likely characteristics of next generation technologies. The Device Technology Working Group considered three technologies most likely to provide the basis for implementation of Petaflops computing systems: advanced semiconductors, optical devices, and superconducting elements. In each case, current capabilities and projected evolutionary advances were explored. From these results, possible roles for each technology in support of Petaflops computers were identified, providing a foundation and constraint space for new system design possibilities. The following summarizes the issues and findings of this working group related to each of the technologies considered. It was found that advanced semiconductor components will provide main memory and possibly processing logic; superconducting technology may provide very high-speed processor logic at very low power consumption; optical technology will provide essential capabilities in high-bandwidth intermodule interconnect and mass storage.

Semiconductor Technologies

The dominant technology in computer manufacture from personal computers to supercomputers for more than a decade has been VLSI semiconductor based on silicon. Continued growth in this technology over that period has led to orders of magnitude improvement in performance, device density, and cost. Other semiconductor technologies, in particular Gallium Arsenide (GaAs), provide alternate operating points than silicon with different trade-offs. The Semiconductor Industry Association (SIA) has developed a detailed projection of the most likely path for semiconductor technology evolution up through the year 2007 [SIA:93a]. Recent examination of the dominant issues has resulted in tentative extensions to the year 2014. These results have proven key to determining viability of Petaflops computing systems within the next two decades and have provided the basis for the Petaflops computer architectures proposed at this workshop.

The state of the art in silicon semiconductor technology employed currently in delivered commercial computers is dominated by feature size which is now approaching 0.5 microns. Current manufacturing yields enable processor chips of half a million gates. DRAMs which provide the bulk of main memory are being delivered with 16 Mbits and SRAMs used for very high-speed memory and caches have up to 4 Mbits. On-chip clock speeds have now reached 200 MHz, although DRAM access times continue to be substantially slower with typical values in the 65 nanosecond range.

The SIA projection shows a steady rate of improvement in most key parameters out to and beyond 2007. It is estimated that at that time, feature size will have reached 0.1 microns. This will enable more than 20 million logic gates to be integrated on a single chip. At that time, DRAM will have a capacity of 16 billion bits and SRAM should be capable of storing 4 billion bits. Advances in clock speed and logic performance will not be so dramatic and is not expected to go much beyond 1 GHz or a clock cycle time of 1 nanosecond. During this time, logic voltages will shrink down to 1.5 volts. Even so, power consumption will be an important issue. It is projected that high-performance integrated circuits may experience power requirements of between 40 and 200 Watts, a significant increase over the 10 to 30 Watt demands of today's high-end processors.

There had been a serious concern that beyond this point in feature size, quantum effects would begin to dominate and new models would be required to estimate progress at finer resolution. However, recent studies have indicated that current trends will continue to feature sizes as small as 0.025 microns by the year 2014. However, it is at this level that semiconductor technology begins to make Petaflops computer architecture viable.

The potential of GaAs is less understood. Significant advances have been made in this technology in the last five years with commercial high-end computers being delivered incorporating GaAs integrated circuits. And new systems employing this technology are being developed. Clocks speeds between a factor of 4 and 10 times that practical with silicon are achievable using GaAs. However device density is measurably less while costs and manufacturing difficulties are significantly more. It is clear that this technology is having an impact on high-performance computer architecture. It is premature to assert that it will become the device technology of choice in the future.

Optical Technologies

Optical technologies offer the potential for significantly increased performance with lower power than semiconductor electronics at least for certain elements of a Petaflops system. This is a consequence of the fundamental differences in the device physics of the two approaches. Unlike electrons, photons do not interact as they cross paths, resulting in a number of desirable properties. Although not as mature as semiconductor technology, optics are already having an impact on medium- to long-range communications and high-density secondary storage. Both these areas have the potential for significant growth leading to critical contributions for Petaflops computing. One area for which optics does not appear to be well suited is in the implementation of logic gates. Thus, while optical technology may be essential for certain critical components, it is most likely to be incorporated in a hybrid architecture integrating two or more distinct technologies.

Optical communications technology for computer module interconnect has emphasized medium- to long-distance paths where its performance benefits over conventional wire-based media offset its current cost disadvantages. As bandwidth requirements increase, optical methods will become favorable for short distances, perhaps even for chip-to-chip interconnect. Optical communication methods exhibit higher bandwidth capacity by orders-of-magnitude than electrical means, and at sufficiently high data rates impose substantially lower energy penalties. These high bandwidth and efficiency advantages are reinforced by optical technology's electrical isolation properties, greatly reducing the possibility of cross-coupling which would otherwise degrade reliability.

There are two primary forms of optical interconnect: guided wave and free-space. Guided wave optical communication employs fiber optics or wave guides to direct light signals between two fixed points. Where line-of-sight paths exist, free-space systems permit high-density space multiplexed signal packing and the potential for path switching and one-to-many broadcast communication.

The state of the art in guided wave optical communication technology provides 100 Megabits per second (Mbps) using light emitting diodes. Recent advances in laser diode emitters has achieved bandwidths of 2.5 Gigabits per second (Gbps). Free space optical interconnects using symmetric, self-electrooptic effect devices have shown the capability of 150 Mbps. High-density, thousand-channel, free-space "fabric" systems have been developed producing throughputs of up to 150 Gbps. Arrays of laser diodes have been fabricated on single semiconductor dies demonstrating the feasibility of electrooptic interfaces and high-bandwidth inter-chip optical communication.

It is projected that within 20 years when Petaflops systems will be feasible, guided wave technology will be capable of providing throughputs on the order of a million million bits per second or 1 terabit per second (Tbps). Using vertical-cavity surface emitting laser diodes, free space methods may reach a capability of 10 million billion bits per second or 10 Petabits per second (Pbps). Not only are these levels of throughput necessary to support Petaflops scale computation, but the added advantage of free space interconnect not requiring the potentially millions of point-to-point wire/fibers to be connected may prove essential for reliability and economic manufacture.

The other area in which optics is expected to have a major impact on Petaflops system design is in the area of memory and mass storage. These take the form of planar and 3D technologies. CD-ROMs and optical tape are the two most common examples of planar optical storage. The consumer level CD optical storage holds somewhat less than 1 Gigabyte and industrial scale optical disks have capacities of up to 20 Gigabytes. Optical tape systems have capacities of between 50 Gigabytes and 1 Terabyte. Access is slow with access times measured in milliseconds for on-line disks and many seconds for tapes and robot-loaded optical disks.

Still at the research stage, 3D optical storage techniques offer the prospect of extraordinary memory capacity and bandwidth at moderate to high access speeds. Techniques such as photorefractive rods, two-photon 3D memory, and spectral hole burning are being pursued in the laboratory. It is projected that within ten years 2-photon holographic techniques with spectral hole burning and acousto-optic scanners will provide memory systems on the scale of 10 Terabytes with bandwidths of one Pbps and access time of a microsecond. Using 2D spatial light modulation, storage capacity of 10 Petabytes may be achievable in 20 years.

Superconducting Technologies

Superconducting device technology offers the prospect of clock speeds one to two orders-of-magnitude faster than competing semiconductor devices and, perhaps more importantly, with power consumption requirements one to two orders-of-magnitude lower. These combined features are both critical to the viability of Petaflops computing and place superconducting components among the key contending technologies considered by the Device Technology Working Group. Detracting from the opportunities afforded by superconductivity are the requirements for maintaining and interfacing a supercooled environment (currently 4 Kelvins) and minimal ongoing U.S. industrial R&D investment in this area. The lack of funding is, as usual, a function of market forces. There is no strong market niche in which superconductive computing devices are essential, although some exotic sensors do operate in this regime. Thus, superconductivity is an example of a potentially important enabling technology for Petaflops computing that currently does not benefit a strong market-driven support base.

Experimental sub-systems employing superconducting technology have demonstrated feasibility of implementing the primary constituents for high-performance computing. Logic, memory, and interconnect devices have been fabricated and exhibit superior performance characteristics compared to their semiconductor counterparts. Logic devices have been implemented using $2\,\mu$m lithography permitting VLSI level chips to be implemented although at an order-of-magnitude lower density than state-of-the-art semiconductor devices. Gate delays are at a few picoseconds permitting a multi-GigaHertz supercomputer processor to be built today. Power dissipation per gate, even at these very high switching rates is on the order of microwatts. RAM chips with 4K bits have been demonstrated with access times of 0.5 nanoseconds. At present, 64 K RAM chips are under development, with access times of 0.1 to 0.2 nanoseconds likely in the near future. Superconducting metallization makes ideal transmission lines with extremely low cross-coupling resulting in very low dispersion and loss. Interchip interconnections for Multi-Chip Modules (MCM) have been designed to support throughputs at between 1 and 10 GHz rates. Many of these advances have been achieved in Japan where a prototype supercomputer processor implemented using superconducting technology is being developed by MITI's Electro-Technical Laboratory (ETL).

One challenge to the effective use of systems incorporating this technology is its interface to ambient temperature external environments. Here, the use of free-space optical interconnects may prove most appropriate providing high data rate paths with no corresponding thermal transport medium. A second problem is the relatively low density of superconducting memory compared to that being realized through semiconductors. Purely superconductive memory is not expected to significantly exceed 64K bits although some indications are that this might be pushed to the Megabit per chip level. This is sufficient for registers, buffers, and caches to be used within a superconducting supercomputer. But a higher density memory technology such as semiconductor must provide main memory for any such system.

Leveraging existing techniques and advancing fabrication methods for superconducting devices should enable the development of a 50 Gigaflops superconducting processor within the next five years. Such a machine would operate at a 10 GHz clock rate and comprise a million gates. Main memory would be semiconductor. Most importantly, the processor itself would dissipate only one watt of power (not including main memory). It is believed that further R&D could enhance the clock speed by another factor of 5 to a 50 GHz rate and reduce the power dissipation by another order-of-magnitude. Such advances might yield a one Teraflops processor dissipating approximately four Watts. This is clearly a candidate for the processing component of a thousand-processor Petaflops computing system.

3.3 Architecture

Architecture is driven by the demands of application computing requirements and enabled by advancing technology. Architecture both structures and balances resources to deliver functionality and performance. The Architecture Working Group investigated the largely unexplored regime of parallel computer architecture at the far reaches of Petaflops performance. Although orders-of-magnitude beyond contemporary experience, key issues of technology, parallelism, latency, bandwidth, size, and cost were examined to determine potential approaches and their respective feasibility. Surprises and uncertainty characterized the results, and in the process some popular assumptions were discarded. In the end, a Petaflops computing architecture was conceived–but its gestation is still uncertain, strongly influenced by exigencies poorly understood and even less well controlled. The results of this inquiry reveal a path, milestones, and decision points that can be used to guide planners and establish early research directions.

State of the Art

The state of the art in parallel architecture is represented by multiprocessors comprised of on the order of a thousand high-end microprocessors (developed for the workstation market) at clock rates of a 100 MHz or more with one to four instructions issued per cycle and 32 Megabytes of main memory per processor. Together, these resources are integrated to form systems with peak performance exceeding 100 Gigaflops with main memory in the tens of Gigabytes. Vector architectures with up to 16 very high-speed, large, and highly pipelined processors produce peak performance above 10 Gigaflops using the fastest available semiconductor technology. SIMD architectures employing more than 10,000 fine-grain processing elements have delivered a few Gigaflops performance at modest cost. The cost of the most powerful machines today is in the range of $50M, including some mass storage and peripherals.

Latency management techniques applied to parallel architecture include (1) caches, cache hierarchies, and cache coherence mechanisms; (2) low-latency computing structures; (3) hardware and software prefetching methods; and (4) rapid context switching, multithreaded techniques. Resource management techniques such as data partitioning and task allocation/scheduling are done almost entirely in software, with much of it performed by the application program itself. Fine-grain parallelism is usually exposed by compile-time analysis and is used for individual processor instruction scheduling in execution pipelines and superscalar processors. Some hardware support for reducing overhead of synchronization, data migration, and message passing has been incorporated. Generally speaking, these systems are difficult to program and optimize.

Barriers

The barriers to significant performance gains beyond a Teraflops include many that are readily apparent. Silicon-based microprocessor clock cycle times range from 40 nanoseconds to 5 nanoseconds. The fastest clocks using gallium arsenide are between 2 and 3 nanoseconds. Increasing clock rates so that cycle times will be below 1 nanosecond is unlikely in the near future because the rate of progress in this area is relatively slow.

Cost is a dominant obstacle. Brute force methods today would result in a Petaflops system estimated to cost hundreds of billions of dollars with reliability problematic and usability anyone's guess. Cost is dominated by memory requirements that, if consistent with previous scaling factors, would require a Petabyte of main memory. In today's technology, this would require 100 million components for the memory alone. More generally, cost is influenced heavily by market forces that determine the types and cost of mass produced devices, both largely beyond the influence of the high-performance computing community.

The diameter of the system measured in clock cycles may be extremely broad by the standards of contemporary parallel computers. Millions of transactions between processors and memory will be active simultaneously, requiring levels of memory bandwidth, latency hiding, and fine-grain parallelism well beyond (by orders-of-magnitude) the current base of experience. Reliability and programming methodologies must be major considerations because either could result in a system that is unusable for practical purposes.

Finally, when planning future directions in computer system design, projections for enabling technologies are a crucial source of constraints and guidance. Anticipating trends in underlying technologies is made more difficult by the extended time frame under consideration and the prospect of requiring technologies in the future, now only at their early stage of development.

Alternatives

The approach taken by the Architecture Working Group was to consider three classes of architecture which were lineal descendants of the most promising approaches being pursued today and to determine their viability. If, after close analysis, none were found to promise a likely path to Petaflops performance, this would expose the need for more avant garde approaches perhaps reflecting a new architecture paradigm. The three architecture models considered were:

1. **Coarse Grain:** A low-latency, shared-memory computer employing hundreds of heavily pipelined processors, each capable of a Teraflops performance.

2. **Medium Grain:** A multiprocessor with tens of thousands of workstation-derived microprocessors, each capable of between 10 and 100 Gigaflops performance. This system would probably include a common global name space so that any processor could address any part of main memory directly. But, because of the anticipated large diameter and memory access time, it will require advanced latency management strategies.

3. **Fine Grain:** A distributed multiprocessor with CPUs and memory co-resident on the same chip to expose high levels of memory bandwidth. Hundreds of thousands of these Processor-In-Memory (PIM) chips would be required because the performance of each would be between 1 and 10 Gigaflops. But, the cost would be much lower because less memory—by an order-of-magnitude or more—would be installed with respect to the other two system types. Undoubtedly, this architecture would have a fragmented address space and off-chip transactions would be expensive.

These three system types impose distinct demands on resources and design and provide different characteristics in terms of behavior, e.g., the same applications probably would not perform optimally on all three of these systems. But, the Architecture Working Group did consider the concept of a heterogeneous system made up of one of each of these types with each providing a large fraction of a Petaflops such that the aggregate peak performance would be equal to a Petaflops. It is expected that such a heterogeneous system would offer better performance to cost than any one of the system types scaled up to a full Petaflops.

Results

As a result of a detailed examination of the issues, technology projections, and alternative architecture structures, the working group produced key findings that should establish the direction for future research leading ultimately to effective Petaflops-scale computation. The major findings were:

1. A Petaflops computer architecture will be feasible in a 20 year timeframe.

2. No new architecture paradigm is required to achieve Petaflops computing. Highly advanced versions of today's multiprocessor architectures, combined with known techniques, should provide the basis for Petaflops computing systems.

3. Memory will dominate in determining system size, structure, and cost. An important finding is that scientific problems employing a Petaflops system will not, in many cases, require a Petabyte of memory, but between an order of magnitude less, thus significantly reducing the potential size and cost of the system.

4. Memory latency and bandwidth will be the most critical factors determining effective performance and will require a radical departure from today's typical methods of processor-memory interaction.

5. The driving factor determining the rate of performance evolution is market forces. These forces, resulting from mass market computing requirements rather than those of high-performance computing, will determine when the necessary components will be available and their functionality.

6. Although semiconductor technology still will be the source of the majority of components, cryogenic superconducting technology may provide the processing rates required for the first and possibly the second

of the architecture types considered. Also, an important consideration is power consumption, which is extremely low for superconducting devices. Optical devices are unlikely to provide high-speed logic but will provide the bulk of the interprocessor and memory bandwidth. A concern is that SIA projections do not extend far enough and extrapolations upon which these conclusions are based are subject to revision.

7. Reliability will be determined largely by parts count and this will be limited by cost factors. System costs will constrain parts (i.e., chips) count to a range of between a hundred thousand and a million. This value is at the high end of today's largest systems but should be manageable through advanced engineering techniques.

Recommendations

The results of the Architecture Working Group provide a basis for establishing directions toward Petaflops computing. However, the findings are tentative and predicated on a number of assumptions. Before these findings influence significant future investment, they should be refined and validated through further study in the near term. Several short-term initiatives should be undertaken to resolve the open questions and address the sources of uncertainty.

Architecture Models The architectures considered should be examined in more detail to elaborate on their constituent elements and resource requirements. This will contribute to increased confidence in our understanding of the nature of these systems and provide the basis for conducting trade-off studies.

SIA Projections The current SIA-provided technology projections extend only to the year 2007, and it was only through extrapolation that the characteristics of the needed technologies were assumed. Investment in further semiconductor/technology projections is needed to improve confidence in the timely availability of the necessary devices. This requires that the SIA study be extended to the year 2014.

Applications Scaling A more complete understanding must be gained of the computational resource requirements imposed by applications executing at the Petaflops level. A series of studies of such scaling characteristics will be essential to verify that the architectures are balanced in terms of the needs of the problems they are intended to support.

3.4 Software Technology

Software technology is the enabling logical medium that matches the functional requirements of the user application programs to the capabilities of the computing system's underlying hardware resources. Ideally, software technology presents a logical interface to the user that facilitates programming while achieving efficient execution. Unfortunately, the realities of contemporary practice in the field of high-performance computing exhibit little of this "virtual machine" methodology. The current status of software technology in support of MPP architectures provides neither ease-of-programming nor effective execution. Rather, programmers have to work very close to the iron to achieve real efficiencies and this happens only after much labor. Considering the challenge of providing software technology support for systems ten-thousand to a hundred-thousand times more powerful than today's most aggressive massively parallel processing systems is daunting and brings in to question its viability.

The impact of software technology on high-performance computing is difficult to quantify with the costs incurred and benefits derived often of an intangible nature. This compares unfavorable with developers of the hardware platforms that can measure key factors of their systems or the applications programmers who can show runtimes achieved. While the time to first run of an application program or the degree of execution efficiency achieved are both severely impacted by the effectiveness and utility of the software tools available, the actual benefits achieved are not measured easily. Yet it is apparent from recent experience that effective application of computing systems at the Petaflops scale will be impossible without fundamental changes in the nature of the support provided. The added complexity of million-way parallelism and distributed wide-diameter systems will overwhelm conventional parallel programming methodologies. Even now, no existing single parallelism model adequately covers the spectrum required by applications today.

Programmers are forced to write their applications in reasonable time that run with mediocre performance or invest heavily in optimization and fine tuning of their programs to realize high performance. Historically, the programmer has been forced to make the trade-off between reducing computing time or reducing programming time. The reasons for this are that system design has not been done with system software in mind, and supercomputers in the past have been treated more as high-cost, special-purpose laboratory instruments than general-purpose, easily applied computing systems. Software technology, what there is of it, has been relegated the job of converting these raw capabilities into delivered value for the users. But the widening gap between hardware-supplied capabilities and the needs of user application programs cannot be addressed by current software technology. Petaflops computing systems will require a new paradigm for software technology and this will come only with a holistic design philosophy incorporating advances in algorithms, hardware, and system software designed to be mutually supportive.

The software for the current generation of 100 Gigaflops machines is not adequate to be scaled to a Teraflops and will likely fail on a Petaflops system. In part, this is due to the "big laboratory instrument" mindset that assumes users are dedicated experts entirely consumed for months with tweaking and fine tuning codes to get it just right. Another reason is that supercomputing software environments are seriously underfunded and underdeveloped—a factor driven by the relatively small market. But the challenges confronting Petaflops systems software go beyond inconvenience and are central to the actual feasibility of that scale of computing. This is because parallel machines suffer from "performance instability"—small changes in the relationship between a user program and the underlying hardware resources which can cause dramatic changes in delivered performance. One aspect of this relates to the increasingly "High Q" nature of the processors used. Near peak performance is delivered by a given processor only if the data and control are set up just right. Otherwise, dramatic performance degradation may result. Another aspect of this relates to the drastically increased system diameter—the number of clock cycles it takes for a logical signal/packet to cross the system—that will be characteristic of the Petaflops computer resulting in very long access latencies. Finally, in order to hide this latency, many millions of transactions will have to be active simultaneously requiring that diverse nested and dynamic forms of parallelism be exploited, something done at best very poorly with current methodologies.

Currently, attention has been focused on message-passing and data-parallel programming models which, with some effort, have proven useful for a narrow class of scientific problems but which neither respond well to the challenges above nor generalize easily to broader irregular and dynamic computations. A fully general programming model is required to expose the diverse modes of parallelism, enable portability across platforms, and provide a common programming framework to which commercial software may be targeted by independent software vendors (ISVs). Economic viability will depend on the widest possible usage of the common programming methodology to leverage commercial investment. Such a model must extend beyond a specific platform and encompass heterogeneous ensembles of computing systems as encouraged and enabled by the emerging national information infrastructure (NII). For example, it can be envisioned that applications will become collections of subprograms logically connected as abstract networks of functionality reminiscent of some object-oriented techniques but conducive to mapping across arrays of systems in a seamless environment. Such a methodology would enable, but not be limited to, large scientific programming. Other multidisciplinary interacting programs not currently available would be supported in this extended framework and made possible by Petaflops computing systems. Without tie-in to commercial investment and development driven by the mainstream computing market, a Petaflops architecture initiative would depend entirely on government funding which could not possibly match the resources being applied to general processing technologies.

Software technology for a Petaflops computing system, as well as for more conventional parallel computers, serves two principal purposes:

- It provides a programming methodology, and
- It manages parallel resources and parallel activities for allocation and scheduling.

There is an important overlap between these two considerations in that the runtime resource management establishes the virtual model that is the logical interface to the hardware for the programming system. The programming methodology supported by the software technology comprises the programming language(s) and libraries as well as the sets of tools used for debugging and optimizing application code. The resource management elements of software technology provide services such as file management, virtual memory page swapping, and network interfacing as well as runtime control such as task scheduling (including process level and light weight threads) and resource allocation, process synchronization, and interprocessor communication.

Programming models in current use on high-performance computers can be categorized as: data parallel, message passing, control flow, functional, and object oriented. Even here, languages and models intermix so that one can program in a data-parallel style using distributed memory message-passing languages or shared-memory, control flow languages. Resource management on big systems tends to be limited in the extreme. Either it lacks in functionality leaving little between the programmer and the iron, or it lacks in efficiency which most programmers will reject thus leaving little between the programmer and the iron. This is a consequence of the fact that sophisticated functionality found at the operating system level expects to manage very coarse-grained objects spending hundreds of microseconds performing its services. Highly parallel systems use medium or fine granularity to provide sufficient concurrency to fully utilize all resources. For static regular and/or loosely coupled problems, hand-crafted codes can yield good results. But this simply substantiates the narrowness and difficulty of effective application programming on today's highly parallel systems.

Tools exist for helping programmers examine the time and state of the application program during execution. But they are not used widely yet, although this is likely to change somewhat in the near future. The major reasons for their lack of impact are programmer intransigence, long learning curve, lack of commonality across platforms, lack of availability on some platforms, inaccuracies, and inadequate functionality. Perhaps more to the point is the gap between what these tools present and what the programmer needs to do to achieve improvements in performance. It is often impossible to appreciate the subtle complexities involved in the relationship between program alteration and changes in system behavior. Resource management software is rudimentary in most cases. Often only one user can use a set of system resources at a time. Resource allocation is usually manual and static with poor or nonexistent locality management. And there is no feedback from system behavior to management mechanisms.

Software technology is both crucial to the success of Petaflops computing and requires substantial advances in the current state of the art and practice to achieve the desired success. Advances must be made in both the areas of machine efficiency and human resource effectiveness.

4 Applications Working Group

4.1 Introduction

The Applications Working Group played two major roles in the workshop. First, the needs of important applications are the motivation for designing and building Petaflops machines. This is discussed in Section 4.2 on general terms. Second, the characteristics of potential Petaflops scale applications can be used to guide the other three workshop activities; devices, architectures, and software for Petaflops computers. Our general findings in this area can be found in Section 4.3.

In Section 4.4, we approach the issues of Sections 4.2 and 4.3 from the point of view of particular applications. Section 4.5 describes algorithmic issues.

4.2 Applications Motivation of a Petaflops Computer Program

We show in Table 4.1 a wide set of applications, which are potential uses of Petaflops machines. We divide these into three major areas:

1. Large Scale Simulations (grand challenges) extrapolated from Teraflops machines. Two sub-classes can be separated.
   - Problem size naturally increases (an example is turbulence where more grid points are needed to increase spatial resolution),
   - Problem size is unchanged but there is a need to increase simulated time (an example is protein dynamics with 10,000 atoms and one needs to achieve millisecond simulated time with $\sim 10^{-14}$ second basic time step).
2. Data Intensive Applications that rely on Petabyte $\rightarrow$ exabyte of primary and secondary storage.
3. Novel Applications.

There is no doubt that these can be used to build a strong case for Petaflops machines. As we discuss in the examples of Section 4.4, many applications require Petaflops, or in some cases higher, performance for realistic results. The need for this performance level follows directly from the physical structure of the problem in some cases, and from the size of the base dataset in others. The following observations qualify and expand these remarks.

1. Our working group did not have the broad expertise to establish the Petaflops motivation in full detail.

2. We can give examples, as described in Section 4.4. However, we recommend that our work be refined by appropriate "domain expert groups."

3. We can note generally that computation is and will be increasingly important in economy, society, education, academic, and U.S. needs to be in the lead in the continuing future—just as it is now with HPCC.

4. One cannot predict the critical applications 10–20 years from now. New national problems will arise, and surely HPCC will be critical in many of them. Most of our exemplars will be important, if not the most important Petaflops scale problems.

5. Many Petaflops scale applications will involve integration of disparate activities and will require changes in current modus operandi. For instance, the NII (and applications such as interactive television) will impact society in a nontrivial way. Agile manufacturing requires database (CAD) simulation, design, analysis, manufacturing, and marketing to be integrated. Petaflops computing enables this, but the multidisciplinary character has implications for hardware, software, and hardest of all, the structure of manufacturing companies.

6. We recommend a program to investigate new algorithms needed by Petaflops scale applications and the special architectural features of Petaflops machines. This is expanded in Section 4.5.

7. Historically new algorithms, new difficulties, and indeed new applications have been identified as one increases power of computer—even by a "mere" factor of 10. This is likely to occur in "all" application areas. Today's typical achieved maximum performance is a Gigaflops. Thus, we expect a set of revolutions or "just" minirevolutions as we extrapolate a factor of 10^6 to Petaflops performance.

Table 4.1: Petaflops Application Areas

A. Biology, Biochemistry, and Biomedicine
- A1   Design better drugs
- A2   Understand the structure of biological molecules (protein folding)
- A3   Genome informatics and phylogeny
- A4   Process data from medical instruments
- A5   Simulate functions of human body
  - Blood flow through heart
- A6   Neural networks in cortex
- A7   Real time three-dimensional biosensor data fusion (the virtual human)
- A8   Analysis of integrated medical database to improve quality and cost of health care

B. Chemistry, Chemical Engineering
- B1   Design and understand nature of catalysts and enzymes
- B2   Simulate new chemical plants and distribution (pipeline) systems

C. Physics
- C1   Understand the nature of new materials
- C2   Simulate semiconductors used in chips
- C3   Design fusion energy system (Numerical Tokamak)
- C4   Simulate nuclear explosions
- C5   Matter transporter (three-dimensional fax and edit)
- C6   Understand properties of fundamental particles (QCD)

D. Space Science and Astronomy
- D1   Evolve the structure of the early universe into the epoch of the current observable world (cosmology)
- D2   Understand how galaxies are formed
- D3   Understand large scale astrophysical systems (stars, gas clouds, globular clusters)
- D4   Understand dynamics of Sun
- D5   Understand collision of black holes and emission of gravitational waves
- D6   Analyze new optical and radio astronomy data to combine data from many telescopes and minimize impact of Earth's atmosphere

E. **Artificial Intelligence**
- E1 New neural network learning and optimization algorithms
- E2 High-level searches of full text databases
- E3 Decipher new military coding methods (cryptography)
- E4 Deep search of game trees for social models and games such as computer chess

F. **Study of Climate and Weather**
- F1 Forecast weather and predict global climate
- F2 Forecast severe storms (tornadoes, hurricanes)
- F3 Study coupling of atmosphere, ocean, Earth use with economic and political decisions
- F4 Integrate models and weather data for optimal interpolation (data assimilation)

G. **Environmental Studies**
- G1 Model flow of pollutants and ground water in the Earth (flow in porous media)
- G2 Model air and water quality and relation to policy
- G3 Model ecological systems
- G4 Analyze data from planet Earth to understand nature and use of land (Earth Observing System)

H. **Geophysics and Petroleum Engineering**
- H1 Analyze three-dimensional seismic data to obtain better well placement
- H2 Model oil reservoir to optimize effectiveness of secondary and tertiary oil extractions
- H3 Analyze models of and data from earthquakes to improve predictions of how and when quakes will occur

I. **Aerospace, Mechanical, and Manufacturing Engineering**
    I1 Build more energy efficient cars, airplanes, and other complex artifacts using computational fluid dynamics, structural analysis, and multidisciplinary optimization for a graph of expected performance and memory needs in the aircraft industry (see Figure 4.1)
    I2 Design new propulsion systems
    I3 Simulate new combustion materials
    I4 Simulate radar signature of new vehicles (stealth aircraft)
    I5 Simulate chips used in new computers
    I6 Simulate electromagnetic properties of high-frequency circuits
    I7 Simulate manufacturing processes
    I8 Optimal scheduling of manufacturing systems

J. **Military Applications**
    J1 Simulate new military sensor and communication systems
    J2 Control military operations with data fusion and spatial reasoning
    J3 Integrate human, online military systems, and computer simulations in exercises (SIMNET)

K. **Business Operations**
    K1 Simulations and complex database analysis for advanced decision support in business and politics
    K2 Support integrated agile manufacturing system
    K3 Dynamic scheduling of air and surface traffic when disrupted by weather and crises
    K4 Control and image analysis for advanced robots
    K5 Economic modeling on Wall Street
    K6 Graphics for digital movies
    K7 Linkage analysis to find correlated records in a database indicating anomalies and fraud in health care, securities, credit card operations, and similar areas
    K8 Analysis of customer data to optimize marketing (market segmentation)

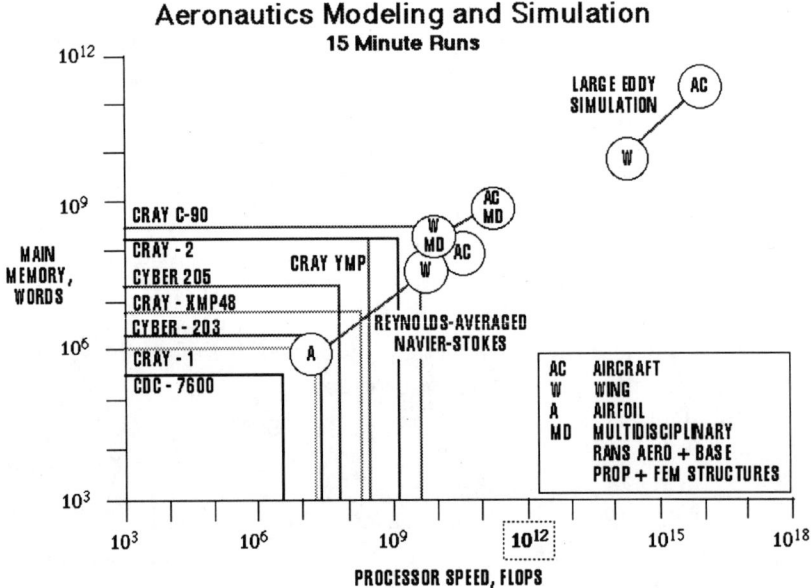

Figure 4.1
Aeronautics Modeling and Simulation

L. **Society**
   L1 Large-scale simulations and database searches for education
   L2 Electronic shopping and other interactive television
   L3 Support world-wide digital library and information systems (text, images, video)
   L4 Integrate and update intelligent agents on the NII (Knowbot garage)
   L5 Image analysis for large databases to find just the right picture (missing persons, cover of magazine)
   L6 Support of up to a million simultaneous players in large virtual environment linked to advanced home video games

4.3 Issues/Characteristics for Architecture (Hardware) and Software of Petaflops Machines

There were particularly fruitful interactions between architecture and application groups. We can make the following general remarks on characteristic features of Petaflops scale applications.

1. We need to establish a common "language" (set of terms) to discuss memory hierarchy/parallelism and communication in a hardware/software /algorithmic implementation neutral fashion. We recommend a near-term activity to refine initial steps begun here to define applications for architecture and software communities. This implementation neutral description of applications and architectures should also help discussions between software and architecture communities. The need for this agreed terminology was highlighted by our discussions with the architecture group where latter noted that application scientists described the computational structure of their problem inappropriately—using, for instance, the language of MIMD distributed memory machines when issues were more general and reflected memory hierarchy. As the target Petaflops machine could have a mix of these architectures, a distributed set of hierarchical memory nodes, translating application scientist specifications into Petaflops designs led to vigorous confused debate.

2. Our discussions with architecture group isolated several classes of machines—three based on memory hierarchy processor trade-offs and others based on memory size and I/O requirements.

3. We made a list of architectural features, which are shown in Tables 4.2, 4.3, and 4.4. These were used as a guide in preparing exemplar application discussions in Section 4.4.

4. We recommend that once a better framework is agreed (see item 1.), that "domain experts" be asked to refine our study (as begun in Section 4.4) in a broader range of potential Petaflops scale applications. Potential application domains are already given in Table 4.1.

5. We identified a general rule for time stepped algorithms (Section 4.4).

$$\text{Memory} = \left[\frac{\text{\# flops}}{1 \text{ Gigaflops}} \right]^n \text{Gigabyte}^*$$

*Put here memory needed at a Gigaflops performance.

Table 4.2
Some General Application Characteristics

---

1. Is Petaflops performance needed by this application, and if so, why?
2. Are new algorithms needed?
3. What are size characteristics of problem? How does size scale as we increase performance of computer?
4. Does this problem have special precision needs?
5. What is nature of computation? Does it involve flops or some other sort of OPS?
6. What are I/O requirements of problem in terms of bandwidth and (secondary) storage size?

$n = 3/4$ for fixed total simulation time, but $n < 3/4$ if needed (as often one does) to increase total simulated time. This rule predicts a memory size of 30 Terabytes is appropriate for a Petaflops machine if 1 Gigabyte is appropriate for a Gigaflops machine. This estimate is consistent with NASA's aerospace predictions in Figure 4.1.

6. Current "rule" memory (bytes) = performance (flops) is modified because up to "now," solving problems has been constrained by machine size and so one scales problem "blindly." On the other hand, the Petaflops machines will solve real problems constrained by the "physics" of the situation.

7. Some interesting characteristics of a Petaflops machine are
   - Petaflops machines will do in five minutes what it takes Gigaflops machines 10 years to do
   - 10^{13} bytes = 8 (bytes/word) × 10 components/grid points × 5000^3 (grid size)
   - 10^{15} bytes = 2300 years video
     $= 10^9$ books
     $= 3 \times 10^8$ Megapixel images
     $= 3 \times 10^{10}$ compressed images

8. Some Petaflops applications are somewhat less demanding on hardware characteristics than today's problems (e.g., they are applications

Table 4.3
Some Architectural Characteristics of Applications

1. What is memory required for a Petaflops performance?
2. What are secondary and tertiary storage needs?
3. Can this application use a metacomputer (networked computers)?
4. Can this application use unconventional architectures (e.g., neural networks, content addressable memory, associative processor)?
5. What is the expected realized versus peak performance for this application?
6. Can this application use a SIMD architecture or a MIMD collection of SIMD "nodes"?
7. Is this application sensitive to latency?
8. What degree of local parallelism is present in this application? This is in addition to "overall" data parallelism and can be exploited in shared memory multiprocessor nodes.
9. How many nodes does "overall" data parallelism support?
  Note: Burton Smith points out that product P of performance (Petaflops) and best possible memory access time (nanosecond) is lower bound to overall concurrency needed in application. P is at least $10^6 (= 10^{15} \times 10^{-9})$. Characteristics 8 and 9 break up this minimal P for a given problem into amount that can be supported by coarse-grain data parallelism (characteristic 8) and that (characteristic 9), which can be exploited in a finer grain (e.g., shared memory) architecture.
10. Discussions with architecture group developed three strawman architectures.
    - Architecture I: Around 200 Teraflops nodes—shared memory architecture
    - Architecture II: Around 10,000 0.1 Teraflops nodes—switch or similar general interconnect
    - Architecture III: Around 10^6 1 Gigaflops nodes—mesh interconnect architecture

    Can applications use these architectures? The answer to this question is related to those of previous characteristics.

Table 4.4
Software Technology Issues for Each Application

---
1. What operating system support does the application need?
2. What compiler and tool support does the application need?
3. Does the application naturally fit particular programming paradigms?
4. Are there special user interface issues?
---

with a lot of compute needs and this implies lower internode communication bandwidth to node compute power ratio).

9. It is interesting to consider real-time applications so that Petaflops performance is required to keep up with the machine and people in loop (e.g., defense simulation and control).

10. Many real-world simulations need Petaflops because problems have multiple length scales.

11. All members of the applications working group felt that Petaflops central supercomputers should be accompanied by the natural scaling Teraflops level workstations distributed among the users.

4.4 Exemplar Applications

Porous Media

From today's machines to the Petaflops computer, there is a factor of 10^4 in speed. How will this produce value in problems of major importance to society?

Most important problems are already solved at some level, but most solutions are insufficient and need improvement in various respects:

- under resolution of solution details, averaging of local variations and under representation of physical details

- rapid solutions to allow efficient exploration of system parameters

- robust and automated solution, to allow integration of results in high-level decision, design, and control functions
- inverse problems (history match) to reconstruct missing data require multiple solutions of the direct problem.

For PDE-based problems, the computational effort scales inversely as grid size to the fourth power, h^4, and often, especially for implicit problems, higher powers, such as h^7 can occur.

For field scale oil reservoir simulation, grids on the order of 100 meter spacing might be common. Geological variation occurs on all length scales, down to the pore size of the rock, about a micron. Not all of this variation needs to be simulated, fortunately. The interwell separation is perhaps 400 meters, and flow between wells is the important variable to be predicted. Variation on the range of 10 to 20 meters is not well represented by averaging methods, and is better computed, so that there is a utility in refining grids by a factor of 5 to 10.

On the basis of these considerations, we propose the following simulation, for which the Petaflops machine would be necessary:

1. $10^3 \times 10^3 \times 10^2 = 10^8$ grid elements
2. 30 species
3. 10^4 time steps
4. 3×10^9 words of memory per case
5. 300 cases considered (geostatistical parameters; economic or operating parameters; history matching iterative solutions of the direct problem)
6. 10^{12} words of memory (all cases considered in parallel)
7. 3×10^{14} grid $\times$ time cells total
8. 10^{19} flops
9. 10^4 sec = 3 hrs. Petaflops computational time

At these length scales, geological data is not known, except in a statistical sense, and so statistical ensemble averages will provide average performance as well as a measure of variability associated with these averages and the possibility or probability of outlier solutions, such as early breakthroughs.

Similar issues apply to ground water remediation sites. Here the sites and well spacings are typically smaller, but the same scaling of grid to well spacing arguments apply. Commonly narrow conduction bands, or isolated time events, such as runoff during storms dominate total migration of contaminants so that accurate resolution in space and time is needed for reliable predictive capability.

Complicated chemistry, included binding of contaminants to absorption sites, or the trapping of contaminant bearing water in semi-isolated micropores gives rise to the disturbing phenomena of sites which appear to be remediated by a pump and treat method, only to have the contaminant re-emerge when treatment is terminated. For this reason, physical processes, and system variables often need an increased accuracy of description, as well as finer grid resolution.

What are the architectural issues which result from this problem?

For memory, we see that memory size is determined almost entirely by the application, and is nearly independent of system architecture. The Petaflops machine is mainly justified to solve large problems, rather than to solve problems of a fixed size more rapidly. For the easiest problems, we have

$$\text{memory} \sim \text{speed}^{3/4}$$

but for many cases, and especially the more computationally difficult ones, the exponent will be smaller, because:

- some of the extra computational power will be devoted to solution for longer total time, or exploration of more parameter values

- for implicit problems, or nonlocal force laws, the computational work grows more rapidly than h^4.

These scaling laws should be developed with known proportionality coefficients coming from today's machines, which appear to be well balanced for a broad mix of problems.

There is a similar scaling law for communication latencies in memory hierarchies. Communication of n bytes takes $an+b$ units of time, where a and b are measured dimensionlessly in units of floating point operations. Here b is latency and a is bandwidth.

The number of floating point operations which can be usefully performed between communication steps is proportional to the local memory size. Consider a two-level hierarchy, with M bytes stored at m locations. After $O(mM)$ floating point operations, there will be a need to communicate $O(m)$ domain decomposition boundary information messages of size $O(M^{2/3})$ in the most favorable case, and $O(m^2)$ messages of size $O(M)$ in the worst case. For the more common favorable case, the communication cost is

$$m(aM^{2/3} + b)$$

and the computational cost is

$$mM$$

so we need

$$mb + maM^{2/3} \ll mM$$

or

$$b \ll M$$

and

$$a \ll M^{1/3}$$

Constants in these relations can be determined from current balanced machines. The same arguments can be extended to multilevel memory in a hierarchy.

In the unfavorable cases, the problem has not been parallelized successfully at a conceptual level, and the machine will fail for these problems in the absence of further algorithmic work. For example, dense matrices may achieve a more nearly sparse character if a better basis is used, such as a multipole or wavelet basis. Such algorithmic methods may move a problem from an unfavorable to a favorable case.

For porous media problems, the pressure is solved implicitly. This problem has a bad condition number as the mesh is refined. Thus, there is a need for preconditioners (approximate solution methods) of a hierarchical nature, to put these problems in the favorable scaling cases. Clearly research issues of a numerical analysis nature will arise.

Computational Astrophysics

Need for a Petaflops Computer There is a wide variety of interesting and challenging problems to be solved in this field which require a correspondingly wide variety of computational techniques and machine capabilities. A partial list of possible applications includes multidimensional stellar evolution—from star formation to the death of the star in a supernova explosion, cosmological simulations, galaxy formation, accretion disk structure and evolution, and the formation of supersonic jets. There are several reasons why these problems will require (at least) a Petaflops computer in order to obtain reliable solutions. One is the need to simulate enormous ranges in length and time scales, requiring very large computational grids (possibly using adaptive mesh techniques) and huge numbers of time steps. Very large grids also are required to reduce the numerical dissipation in order to represent accurately the extremely low viscosity of most astrophysical gases. This is particularly important in regimes where turbulence and convective motions are important. Most problems will require fully three-dimensional simulations. Calculations containing 10^9 grid points or more will have to be done routinely. Many problems will require complex physics calculations at each grid point, such as nuclear reaction networks involving perhaps hundreds of species and thousands of reactions, detailed equation of state calculations, complex radiative transfer, and solution of elliptic equations to calculate, for example, self gravity. Calculations of galaxy formation will require coupling of a gas dynamics code to an N-body code to follow the motions of individual stars. Finally, it will be necessary to run each simulation many times to fully understand the physics of the object(s) being studied. These additional simulations will involve parameter studies, modifying the initial conditions, using different input physics, and so on.

Architectural Issues The applications in this field can be divided into two major classes, those that require global communications and those that need only local communications. Applications requiring only local communications involve explicit gas dynamics on regular grids with only zero-dimensional microphysics, such as reaction networks and equation of state calculations at each grid point. Applications which use global communication include implicit gas dynamics methods, adaptive grids, radiative transfer, self-gravity calculations, and N-body tree codes. These two set of applications have somewhat different machine requirements, which will be addressed separately below.

For applications which use only local communications, virtually any number of processors would be used. Certainly 10^6 processors would present no significant difficulty and perhaps even 10^9 processors could be used effectively on some applications. Only nearest neighbor communications would be involved and a sufficiently large number of operations can be done at each grid point between communications steps that issues of latency and communication bandwidth become less critical. Applications of this type should run efficiently on any balanced architecture and obtain a significant fraction of peak speed.

For applications requiring global communications, computers with a smaller number of faster processors will be easier to use. These applications also will require faster communications with lower latency to run efficiently. It seems unlikely that these applications will achieve a large fraction of peak speed using conventional hardware and software approaches. There is a high probability that applications in this class will become increasingly important in the future as algorithms for multi-dimensional implicit gas dynamics, multidimensional radiative transfer, and adaptive grids become more popular.

I/O and Memory Requirements Consider a reasonable problem size using a 1000^3 grid. Assuming a few hundred variables per grid point, the calculation would require 1–10 Teraflops of memory. Typically, one would like to store the values of each variable at least 1,000 times during the calculation, which would require approximately 10 Petabytes of data storage. If this calculation could be completed in 10 hours of cpu time, the required I/O speed would be one Petabyte per hour. This should be considered as only a representative example, and is certainly not an extreme case. Many simulations will require significantly more capabilities than this, particularly in the areas of storage and I/O speed.

Lattice QCD

Lattice QCD is a perfect problem for simple parallel computer architectures. High efficiency is very easy to reach. The Petaflops threshold will allow a dramatic change in the scope of numerical simulations of lattice QCD, which will become a really effective phenomenological tool and support to experiments. Weak interaction physics will be understood in a seriously quantitative way, and it will be possible to compute scattering amplitudes with high precision. Experiments like the one that are planned in this period (beauty and phi factories) will be able to exploit such a powerful help (quantitative predictions from the microscopic theory, without approximations).

As we already said, numerical simulations of lattice QCD can have very high efficiency even on very simple architectures. The problem is computationally intensive, since one always operates on complex 3×3 matrices: a low cpu memory bandwidth is acceptable. Since one is simulating a virtual world, and only needs to write on disk a few average numbers (apart from backups and check points), a powerful I/O channel is not needed. The problem is local and homogeneous, and the mapping to processor architecture straightforward. The cost-effective mesh architecture of Class III in Table 4.3 seems satisfactory. Further, a reasonable 200^4 lattice requires around 10 Terabytes of memory to match a Petaflops performance. Larger problems than this would require major new algorithms such as the multiscale renormalization group.

Computational Quantum Chemistry—HIV Protease Structure

Petaflops will have many applications studying the electronic structure of macromolecules, clusters, surfaces, and solids. Here, we discuss an example: The structure and properties of HIV protease by means of *ab initio* quantum chemical methods.

The detailed electronic structure of the HIV protease molecule can be elucidated using methods based on Hartree-Fock theory and its extensions (post-Hartree-Fock theory) such as configuration interaction and many-body perturbation theory. Using present day computers, application of these theories to such biological molecules is prohibitively expensive at the lower levels of approximation and become intractable as higher levels are used. These and related methods of *ab initio* quantum chemistry utilize the complete nonrelativistic Hamiltonian operator for a system comprised of N electrons and M nuclei and require the calculation of integrals involving kinetic energy, nuclear attraction and nuclear repulsion operators [Mulliken:81a].

The Hartree-Fock-Roothaan (HFR) procedure is used in most present day *ab initio* applications to polyatomic systems. It, or components thereof, also can be used as a point of departure for post-Hartree-Fock methods. HFR calculations use basis sets to define one-electron orbitals in the construction of molecular orbitals (MOs) as linear combinations of atomic orbitals (LCAOs). The basis functions are usually Gaussian-type functions (GTFs) centered at the atomic nuclei for a polyatomic system. For an m basis function representation of the N electrons in the system, the HFR procedure results in a total of $(m^2 + m)/2$ kinetic energy, $(m^2 + m)/2$ nuclear attraction, and $(m^4 + 2m^3 + 3m^2 + 2m)/8$ electron repulsion integrals. Although the $O(m^2)$ one-electron integrals is manageable with current computing technologies, the $O(m^4)$ scale-up of the two-electron integrals soon exhausts the capabilities of even the most advanced massively parallel processing supercomputers—in spite of the fact that the computation of such integrals (matrix elements) is "embarrassingly parallel" [Harrison:93a].

At the Hartree-Fock level, the $O(m^4)$ integrals are assembled into a Fock matrix of order n (where n equals the number of contracted GTFs; refer to example below) and its eigensolutions are extracted. This process is repeated over and over until solutions are invariant to within a pre-chosen threshold (i.e., attain self-consistency). Typically, this can require hundreds of iterations. A benchmark is a HFR calculation on a cluster of 135 beryllium atoms represented by a $(3s2p)/[2s1p]$ basis set of contracted GTFs [Ross:94a]. (The larger basis of 3 s-type and 2 p-type "primitive" GTFs is collected, using fixed coefficients derived from free-atom calculations, into the smaller "contracted" set of 2 s-type and 1 p-type GTFs for computational efficiency [Mulliken:81a].) The Be_{135} basis set contains $m = 1215$ primitive and $n = 675$ contracted GTFs. The $O(m^4)$ integrals step ($\sim 10^{12}$), which was reduced significantly using molecular point group symmetry, consumed 24 CRAY X-MP cpu hours.

Biological molecules such as HIV protease contain approximately $O(1,500)$ nuclei and $O(5,000)$ electrons. A modest, but not unreasonable, basis set could contain 10,000 basis functions. Simple scaling of the Be_{135} result indicates that it would require $\sim$ 30 cpu years on the approximately 1 Gigaflops CRAY X-MP to calculate the required 10^{16} two-electron integrals. This calculation reduces to a very tractable 15 minutes on a Petaflops computer.

To determine the equilibrium structure of HIV protease using Hartree-Fock theory would require repeating this 15-minute calculation for different molecular geometries until the total energy reaches a minimum. Since there are nearly 4,500 vibrational degrees of freedom, an unrestricted geometry search scaling roughly as the number of nuclei squared becomes prohibitive even on a Petaflops computer. Fortunately, it is appropriate to focus on the active site of the molecule and restrict the atomic motions to the few in its vicinity. The problem of geometry variation then can be addressed in hours to days.

Reactions and interactions at the active site are of particular interest in HIV protease. Because chemical bonds are formed and cleaved, it may be necessary to use higher levels of approximation than Hartree-Fock theory to calculate accurate results. Configuration interaction and many-body perturbation theory approaches can be used in such cases [Mulliken:81a]. A requirement for these post-HF methods is the so-called four-index transformation of the $O(m^4)$ basis function (contracted GTF) integrals to the MO basis—an $O(m^5)$ process [Covick:90a]. This step is followed in the configuration interaction (CI) procedure, for example, by construction of the Hamiltonian matrix comprised of elements connecting excitations or configurations involving so-called virtual MOs. In a full-CI procedure, the order L of the Hamiltonian matrix grows roughly as m^N for a configuration space of m MOs containing N electrons. In the case of HIV protease, this is $L = 10,000^{5000}$ configurations, a calculation that would take an inconceivable length of time. A more feasible procedure would be to treat at the CI level only those electrons in the vicinity of the active site. In this instance, the CI procedure becomes tractable and the calculation may be limited by the $O(m^5)$ transformation step. Furthermore, the excitation levels could be constrained to replacements of electrons from occupied to virtual MOs in order of $i = 1, 2, 3, \ldots$ for single, double, triple, etc., excitations. The CI calculation then scales roughly as m^i. The lowest energy eigensolutions of the $O(L)$ Hamiltonian matrix must be calculated—a formidable task even for a Petaflops computer handling a CI that scales as m^i because L is still greater than 10^8.

The discussion presented here clearly infers that the advent of Petaflops computing will lead to an unprecedented expansion in the scope of *ab initio* quantum chemistry. Biological systems such as HIV protease, which are currently impossible to study at any level of theory using today's state-of-the-art computers, will become rote using HFR methods on a Petaflops machine. And despite the fact that highly accurate full-CI calculations will remain out of reach, the feasibility of post-Hartree-Fock methods will no longer be an unattainable goal. Consequently, the advent of Petaflops supercomputing will result in the birth of *ab initio* quantum biochemistry and the coming of age of *ab initio* quantum chemistry.

Petaflops or Petaops Requirements from Genome Projects

The Human Genome project should produce the entire sequence of all 3×10^9 bases of human DNA in the next decades. It is reasonable to expect that in that same time frame it may be possible to do genomes of similar size, such as individual humans, experimental and domestic animals, crops, and others at the rate of one per year. Rates of 100 bases per second may be routine. Full, element-by-element comparisons of new sequences with existing data bases would require more than 10^{11} to 10^{12} elementary comparisons per second, compounded as the database grows. Clever heuristics can reduce the essential operations, but a newly discovered method could require complete re-analysis of all existing data. Full comparison of human and mouse genomes would need 10^{18}–10^{19} operations. This kind of comparative sequence analysis is already one of the most powerful sources of knowledge about genes, and shows promise of becoming more important as the data and knowledge bases grow. These discoveries will drive the need for even more sophisticated analyses.

Genomic information completely determines the characteristics of the protein and nucleic acid molecules that express a living organism's form and function. One of the greatest challenges, in which computation is playing a major role, is the prediction of higher-order structure from the one-dimensional sequence of genes. Rules for prediction of macromolecule folding are beginning to emerge. In the case of RNA, there are some simple rules that partially predict the secondary interactions of distant parts of the polymer chain. A deterministic, dynamic programming code is in wide use. It scales as $\sim N^3$ in operations and $\sim N^2$ in memory. Other non-deterministic methods also are available. More complex methods for predicting three-dimensional structure are appearing. Preliminary secondary structure predictions for sequences of HIV RNA (9,218 nucleotides) can be done on a 16 K processor SIMD Maspar or an 8-processor CRAY Y-MP in about six hours. There are 100,000s of sequences of potential interest ranging in size from 50 to 10,000 nucleotides.

Protein structure prediction is even of greater interest since proteins are the principal agents of expression for genetic information. Rules for prediction are more complex that for RNA, and are a research area of major concern. In its extreme, the problem could be viewed as of n^N complexity, where reasonable values for n, the number of conformations amino acids may take, could be dozens. Exhaustive conformational search would not be feasible for many proteins, even with Petaflops computers. However, even now there are a number of strategies to explore the problem. Exhaustive search on highly simplified lattice models, using simplified potential functions is partially successful. Statistics-based assignments of structure from sequence similarities is another. In all cases, refinement of final structures requires molecular mechanical and computational chemistry tools.

Much experimental work, involving heavy computation, is still needed in algorithm development for both the RNA and protein-folding problem.

Problem match to three categories of Petaflops computer: Almost every sort of high-performance architecture is easily adaptable to sequence comparison. Workstations are very competitive at the present time.

Class I machines are seldom used for sequence matching. High-precision word length is not needed. Lattice models are explored with supercomputers for their raw, scalar speed. Three-dimensional modeling is most frequently done on scalar plus vector, and limited multiprocessor shared memory.

Class II machines will do well on sequence comparison. Some HPCC efforts are adapting the molecular mechanical and electronic methods.

Class III machines are beginning to appear for sequence matching in commercial products. Some experimental adaptations of molecular mechanics calculations on heterogeneous architectures have been done.

Drug Design

Current costs of developing a new drug are several hundred million dollars. Good candidates are scarce. For example, by screening 10s to 100s of thousands of natural products and other chemicals, new anticancer agents emerge at less than one per year. Computation is anticipated as a powerful aid to designing and prescreening new candidates. This approach requires fundamental structural data on potential targets and the agents that may affect them. High-performance computer models are essential for analysis of experimental structural data to produce detailed molecular models, to molecular mechanical/dynamic exploration of target structures, to chemical structure of small drugs, and to interaction between drugs and targets. All of these methods will require Petaflops capability to achieve reliable prediction, design, and testing.

Structure determination requires computation in solution of the phase problems of x-ray crystallography and in distance geometry calculation for magnetic resonance. Computational chemistry is needed to understand the structure of drugs, how they bind to targets at the atomic level, and for details of electronic structure.

As examples, consider the protease of HIV and its inhibitors. This enzyme is required for mature, infectious virus to be produced, and is thus a candidate for drug targeting. It is being studied extensively. At this stage, computing speeds are on the order of 10^{12} fold slower than desired. Typically, 10^{-9}s of real time requires 100 CRAY Y-MP hours. We want to cover 1 ms of chemical time.

Petaflops performance would permit electronic calculations for the entire protease (at moderate levels of theory) and very detailed calculations for drug-sized molecules.

The calculations currently scale as N^2 for number of atoms in molecular mechanics calculations, with various heuristics to reduce from this upper bound. Electronic structure requirements vary depending on the level of theory, but range from N^4 upward. Memory requirements scale as N^2 for molecular mechanisms with additional offline storage for molecular dynamics trajectories. Electronic structure codes vary in memory requirement depending on whether storage and re-use of intermediate values or recomputation is chosen.

Problem match to three categories of Petaflops computers:

Class I—These codes traditionally are heavy users of Class I machines. Vectorization and multiprocessing are not high. Memory use is significantly less than 1 MW/MF for molecular mechanics and can be less or more than 1 MW/MF for electronic calculations.

Class II—Current codes are being ported to predecessor machines of this class. Managing communication is a significant effort.

Class III—A few demonstrations have been done on SIMD machines that may be analogous to Class III architectures.

Three-Dimensional Heart

The challenge is to develop a realistic three-dimensional model of the heart for improved design of prosthetic heart valves, modeling of cardiac diseases, and understanding the functional anatomy of the heart.

Petaflops are needed to allow current promising models to be scaled to realistic levels of detail.

The present level of development successfully models some portions of the fluid dynamics of a heartbeat. It models the heart as geodesic fiber paths on surfaces in three dimensions, based on painstaking anatomical dissection of mammalian hearts. Fiber forces are transmitted to the blood by a special weighting function. Blood is represented currently by $128 \times 128 \times 128$ three-dimensional lattice of points on which fluid dynamics are calculated using versions of the Navier-Stokes equations. The problem scales in memory as slightly less than the grid size cubed, and in computational complexity as more than N^4. Present requirements are a CRAY C90 cpu-week and 50 Megawords of memory for a single beat. Realistic improvements would require a Petaflops computer, and could be utilized immediately to refine the many parameters, to achieve steady-state dynamics, and to introduce new features such as electrical activity. Methods developed for this work are applicable to problems of sperm motility, platelet aggregation, and other problems with flexible boundaries, such as blood vessels of the lung and heart.

Problem match to three categories of Petaflops computer:

Class I machines could be utilized immediately. Very large shared memory, vectorizable, multiprocessor codes are in use. The ratio of Megawords to Megaflops is less than one and a high fraction of theoretical peak speed is attained.

Class II machines are likely to be useful with modification of the codes currently being developed on clustered microprocessor machines.

Class III machines are likely to be applicable as well, since they appear to be successful for other fluid dynamics codes.

Global Surface Database

The goal of this application is to create and maintain a database of the surface coverage of the land mass of the Earth at a resolution of 10×10 square meters with samples acquired a few times per days. This database would be able to answer questions like:

- What is the expected quality and yield of this coming year's French wine? This estimate is to be based on the size of the fields being cultivated for grapes, the health of the vines, how they are being fertilized and irrigated, and so on.

- What is the likelihood of food riots in Mongolia this winter? In addition to crop health, need to determine the levels of water reservoirs, the quality of the water, how much fertilizer is being applied, and so on.

- Which forested areas are most susceptible to fires? How dry are the trees, and so on.

- How is energy use distributed in a city? How does usage vary with time of day, changes in weather, and so on?

To answer questions of this type, we propose a database of the surface coverage of the Earth. The land area of the Earth is 1.5×10^{14} meter^2. Dividing the land area in to 10×10 meter^2 grids, yields 1.5×10^{12} grid points.

We assume that each grid point is represented by a sample consisting of a $10^3 \times 10^3$ pixel images, where each pixel is contains intensity information (8 levels) at each of eight different frequencies. (Each pixel corresponds to a single square centimeter.) The image associated with each grid point consists of 6.4×10^7 bits. Further assume that the data can be compressed by a factor of 100; therefore, in compressed form, the data associated with each grid point will be 6.4×10^5 bits.

Satellite downlink characteristics. If 100 satellites are used for image gathering, with downlinks of 10^9 bits per second, we can transmit 1.6×10^5 images per second, or about 1.35×10^{10} images per day. Each grid point will be sampled approximately once every three to four months.

A typical wheat farm (10^4 acres or 4×10^7 square meters) consists of 4×10^5 grid points. Thus we would collect, on average, 3,668 images per day that pertain to the entire farm. In order to determine properly the state of the crops, it will be necessary to look at samples at different times during the day. Thus, the data we will have available for this farm is the equivalent of approximately 600 grid points sampled once every four hours, and from this data we are to determine the health of a field of 10,000 acres.

	Downlink rate	Grid points	percent	Modeled bits
per second	1.0×10^{11}	1.56×10^5	0.00%	8.30×10^7
per day	8.64×10^{15}	1.35×10^{10}	0.91%	7.18×10^{12}
per year	3.16×10^{18}	4.93×10^{12}	331%	2.62×10^{15}

Figure 4.2
Data Rates in Surface Model

Data processing requirements. The compressed data stream produced by satellites is 8.6×10^{15} bits per day. Two steps need to be taken to convert this information into a form appropriate for queries: (1) some signal processing of the image data needs to be performed, and (2) the image at each grid point needs to be converted into information indicating the type of ground cover (wheat, rice, rock, etc.), and the state of the ground cover (dormant, germinating, ready for harvest, etc.). This final form we call a *model*, which consists of an identifier and a state. It is this form that is of most use to those making queries of the database. Since perfect matches with models will be rare, the database will need to associate with each grid point several "closest matching models." For simplicity, we assume that there will be 10^5 different identifier/state combinations, and that 32 closest matching models will be retained for each grid point.

The resulting data rates generated by the satellites are summarized in Figure 4.2. Notice that if the down link rates per satellite were increased to 10^{11} bits per second, nearly every grid point could be sampled each day.

The signal processing typically will require computing the Fourier transform of the image and performing some filtering operations on the resulting set of spectral coefficients. Using some distance metric, these filtered spectral coefficients then are compared against a table of spectral coefficients for different identifier/state combinations and "closest matching models" are selected.

For simplicity, we assume that the signal processing required is a small integer multiple of the cost of performing a Fourier transform of the image attached to each grid point. Each of these images is a $10^3 \times 10^3 \times 8$ array of intensities. Assuming an n point fast Fourier transform takes $n \log n$ floating point operations, the signal processing required per grid point is 8×10^7 flops. Since the satellites can transmit 1.56×10^5 images per second, we will need roughly 1.25×10^{13} floating point operations per second just to perform the basic signal processing. This computation, however, is highly parallelizable and requires little inter-processor communication, since each image can be processed independently.

For template matching, we need to match against 10^5 total models. Each grid point consists of 8×10^6 spectral coefficients, and the distance between these coefficients and the corresponding coefficients of each model must be computed. Using the simple minded approach of computing the distance between the image and each of the models will require a total of 8×10^{11} operations for each grid point. Since 1.56×10^5 images are provided by the satellites each second, 1.25×10^{17} comparisons will be required per second. Without improving the comparison algorithm, this dominates the signal processing cost. Again this computation is highly parallelizable. Storing the data required by the 32 closest matching models will require 532 bits.

A database consisting of one set of 32 models per grid point would require 7.92×10^{14} bits. The satellites will produce 7.18×10^{12} model bits per day (since not every grid point is modeled each day). Thirty years of modeled data will require 9.8×10^{15} bits of modeled data, or one Petabyte.

It is not sufficient to preserve the transformed (modeled) versions of the data. Over time, improved templates will be developed and it then will be useful to re-do the template matching. Each day, the data produced by the satellites in compressed grid point images is 8.4×10^{15} bits. The raw data produced by the satellites over a 30-year period is at least 1.18×10^{19} bits, or one exabyte.

Database Queries. Queries of the global surface database will be made by agricultural planners, economic planners, city planners, climate modelers, sociological studies, political studies, etc. We anticipate upwards of 10^6 queries per day or 12 queries per second, each query requiring correlations over varying regions of the database.

The processed database is approximately 10^{15} bytes. Some queries will use substantial portions of the database and the queries will need

	N cost	$N \log N$ cost	N^2 cost
All archived data	1.14×10^{17}	6.04×10^{18}	1.12×10^{33}
U.S. data, one sample/grid	5.73×10^{14}	2.61×10^{16}	1.12×10^{28}
Farm 10^4 acres	4.68×10^6	8.72×10^7	1.90×10^{12}

Figure 4.3
Query processing time in operations per second

to be answered on the order minutes. (For reference, the United States is 1/16 of the land mass of the planet.) A query that needs access to the entire database in five minutes would require a bandwidth of 32.8 Terabytes per second. Accessing a single model set for each grid point in the United States in five minutes requires bandwidth of 165 Gigabytes per second.

The table in Figure 4.3 estimates the computational cost required for different classes of queries. It is assumed that 10^6 queries per day are to be processed and each is identical. Three different size queries are estimated: (1) one that uses the entire data contained in the database, (2) one that uses the data corresponding to one sample for each grid point in the United States, and (3) one that uses the data corresponding to one sample for each grid point on a 10^4 acre farm. In addition, it is assumed that the computation required to handle the query is either linear, $n \log n$, or quadratic.

Clearly, Peta-operation machines will have difficulties with these query rates if a query requires more than linear processing. However, even large-scale queries that deal with all of the archived information can (barely) be handled by Peta-machines if efficient (linear) algorithms can be developed.

Video Image Fusion

Description: This application combines real-time video or other image sensor data with solids models of an object or complex physical system to create a CyberScene. This combined dataset provides users an immersive virtual environment that can be explored in real time. Typical applications include exploration via telepresence of dangerous, small or large scale or otherwise inaccessible physical locations for example, reactor cores, deep sea vents, manufacturing floors, inside of human body, etc. A system with 10^3 high-resolution (10^6 pixel) input video streams (these video or other arrayed sensor data most likely will come from highly integrated array cameras) requires a Terabit per second (Tbps) of input bandwidth and would be used to computationally reconstruct a 10^{12} voxel 3D CyberScene object. This object will be merged with any available CAD or solid model of the physical system. These CAD or solids models may be based on 3D laser scans or other active scanning databases but we do not consider the data or computational requirements for active scanning here. We estimate real-time voxel reconstruction to require on the order of a 10^5–10^6 floating point operations per voxel per second and 10–10^2 communications events. Communications events are needed for merging multiple pixels into a single 3D pixel (voxel). Existing 3D image reconstruction systems are limited to a small number of depth planes; therefore, we increase the number of input sources to improve the number of depth planes in the final reconstructed 3D image to provide uniform spatial resolution of the CyberScene. Output bandwidth requirements depend on the number of users. We estimate 100 users would require a Tbps of output bandwidth to provide for 100 high-resolution 3D immersive displays (CAVE or high resolution head mounted displays).

System Requirements: This application requires a Petaflops computer system with between 10^3 and 10^5 processors. Global communication is required since voxel reconstruction requires parallel FFTs and/or wavelets and correlation and registration of multiple image planes. Global communication is required for image registration; global sums are needed for FFTs, correlation, etc. Total primary storage of $\sim 10^{15}$ bytes is required. Multiple seconds of image data are required to be in primary storage for motion estimation while motion parallax extraction requires $O(10^{14})$ bytes, and underlying 3D solids model will require $O(10^{14})$ bytes, and additional primary memory is needed for buffer space for secondary store. The Petaflops system requires significant real-time I/O capability both for user data streams but also for archival storage of cyberspace events. Secondary storage will be used for both archiving input directly, but also for recording and playback of events (e.g., multiple Tbps to secondary store is needed). Secondary store capacity needs to be in the range of 10–100 Petabytes. The algorithms for CyberScene reconstruction can use computer systems with rather deep memory hierarchies; however, it is not clear that this application can make use of SIMD architectures.

Impact: CyberScene capability can have a broad economic impact. The potential uses include: telepresence for dangerous environment work (reactors, contamination zones, biological hazards and deep sea construction, mining), simulation and training of workers for complex manufacturing environments (highly automated assembly lines), entertainment and education, mass participation in remote space exploration activities (space station, lunar and mars based environments), 3D high-end telecommuting, and merging of VR with RR.

4.5 Algorithmic Issues for the Petaflops Computer

Algorithms sit between the application and the machine and interact with both. Advances in the performance and architecture of the machine may have a serious impact on the choice of algorithms and vice versa.

The main algorithmic issue in going from a Teraflops machine to a Petaflops machine is *scalability* (because the problems to be solved on the latter will be necessarily much larger), in terms of both the algorithmic efficiency (i.e., the serial complexity of the algorithm) and the parallelization efficiency. Unfortunately, these are often two conflicting goals.

We list, in Table 4.5, three different types of algorithms viewed in these two terms:

We expect a Petaflops machine to have two essential features that will influence critically the proper choice of algorithms: the memory will be hierarchical (in terms of access time) and the processor interconnect will be hierarchical (e.g., a MIMD network of SIMD machines). We expect that these architectures will favor algorithms that are also hierarchical in nature, because there will be a better match in terms of the algorithm's demand for synchronization/communication and the efficiency with which the machine can deliver them. For example, for elliptic PDEs, a hierarchical architecture should favor hierarchical algorithms such as multigrid and domain decomposition. These types of algorithms

Table 4.5
Characteristics of General Algorithm Classes

Type of Algorithm	Example	Algorithm Scalability	Parallel Scalability
Local/regular	PDE time marching	poor	good
	Monte Carlo	poor	good
global	Pseudo time stepping	poor	good
	Sparse matrix inversion	poor	poor
	Multigrid	good	not optimal
dynamic/irregular	Local mesh refinement	good	poor

require both local and global data interaction but the amount of interaction decreases with the distance between the processors. Such an architecture may also favor a preconditioned iterative approach where the preconditioner can be chosen to better match the architecture.

On the other hand, a potential problem is that it is often difficult to implement hierarchical algorithms to run at perfect parallel efficiency. A Petaflops machine will necessarily involve a large degree of parallelism and it may increase the percentage of time an algorithm spends on synchronization and communication (the Amdahl's Law effect). For example, on the coarser grids, there are fewer data to keep the machine busy. Much more research is needed, both in new algorithms that parallelize across grid levels and also in architectures that do not impose a heavy penalty for these kinds of multilevel communication patterns.

Another issue is problem scalability. For some problems, the scale-up in the size of the problem does not give rise to increased parallelism. For example, in certain molecular dynamics applications, one may want to fix the number of molecules but increase the number of time steps. Unfortunately, it is difficult to extract parallelism in the time direction. We may need to develop better algorithms to deal with these kinds of problems.

A final issue is precision. We may need to increase the precision as the problem size grows. For example, for many elliptic PDE problems, the conditioning grows like $O(n^2)$ (2nd-order problems) or $O(n^4)$ (4th-order problems), where n is the number of grid points in each co-ordinate direction. Therefore, for $n = 10^4$, a 4th-order elliptic solver may not have any accurate significant digits on current 64-bit word machines. A Petaflops machine may need to have increased precision. Alternatively, more stable and better conditioned discretizations can be employed. For example, Monte Carlo methods are less sensitive to precision than those based on solving differential equations. Further, such statistical methods are often straightforward to parallelize. Thus, we anticipate that further investigation of Monte Carlo algorithms may be important for Petaflops scale applications.

4.6 Acknowledgments

Chair:

Geoffrey C. Fox	Syracuse University
	gcf@npac.syr.edu

Associate Chair:

Rick Stevens	Argonne National Laboratory
	stevens@mcs.anl.gov

Working Group:

Tony Chan	University of California at Los Angeles
Dwight Duston	BMDO
Walter Ermler	U. S. Department of Energy
Jim Fischer	NASA Goddard
Bruce Fryxell	NASA Goddard
Ed Giorgio	U. S. Department of Defense
Jim Glimm	SUNY, Stony Brook
Jacob Maizel	National Institutes of Health
Rob Schrieber	NASA RIACS
Paul Stolorz	Jet Propulsion Laboratory
Francis Sullivan	Supercomputing Research Center
Richard Zippel	Cornell University

5 Device Technology Working Group: Semiconductor, Optical, and Superconductive Devices

5.1 Introduction

The Device Technology Working Group addressed three major areas of device technology: semiconductor, optical, and superconductive; and examined the emerging areas of neural networks and single electron transistors. The working group explored the three device technologies with respect to current state-of-the-art trends in research and development, projections about device capabilities by the year 2014, and barriers and obstacles to achieving the requisite performance levels for Petaflops computing.

The feasibility of a Petaflops machine depends on the availability of high-performance processor and memory devices. Assuming some focused research initiatives, projections of future semiconductor device technologies indicate that Petaflops computing machines can be supported. In addition, where feasible the group developed specific recommendations about research and development areas that need new or enhanced funding and direction.

5.2 Silicon Device Technology

Devices resulting from evolutionary progression of complementary metal oxide semiconductor (CMOS) technology are most likely to be used in Petaflops systems. CMOS dominates current device technology, and enjoys very high levels of continuous world-wide investment. It is pervasive with an infrastructure in place to support every aspect of research, development, design, and application. Also, the technology is sufficiently well understood that future device capabilities can be predicted with only modest risk. Asserting the merits of CMOS, however, is not a recommendation to ignore other device approaches. Research and development over the next two decades will result in new high-performance device technologies which may be well suited for Petaflops computing systems. Proposed alternative approaches will be measured against the CMOS option, and they must show significant advantages over CMOS to be given serious consideration.

The working group explored expectations for deep submicrometer feature size CMOS devices and identified the 0.05 micrometer technology generation as capable of supporting Petaflops machines in about the 2015 time frame. Also, it is possible that Petaflops machines can be built earlier using larger feature size technology—if circuit design and architectural schemes provide added performance. Using the 0.05 micrometer technology as a reference point, the viability of the physical, electrical, and thermal aspects of a Petaflops machine were considered.

The potential for using future CMOS technology to build Petaflops machines was examined in four phases. First, the characteristics of existing and emerging processor devices were reviewed. Second, the scope of existing technology predictions was evaluated. Third, focused scaling and engineering judgment device predictions were developed. Finally, the utility of the predicted device technology for Petaflops machines was examined.

Existing Silicon Devices

An important factor to remember in discussing present day devices is that they represent one sample point about 70% of the way through an approximate 17-year life cycle. A technology generation goes through three phases of maturity: a seven-year research period, a five-year development period, and a five-year manufacturing period. For any given generation, identifying when one period ends and another begins is difficult, and devices from different technology generations co-exist in time.

Leading-edge microprocessors being shipped today were introduced in the1992–1993 time period. Fabrication technology minimum feature size ranges from 0.8 micrometers down to 0.6 micrometers. In 1994, processors will be introduced that exploit 0.5 micrometer technology. About a two-year lag exists between the technology roadmap year and the actual introduction of the technology in a microprocessor product. Current commercial device complexity, measured in terms of transistor count, is about 3 million transistors per chip. The Intel Pentium and the TI Super Sparc are at the high end with 3.1 million transistors, and the IBM/Motorola PowerPC 601 follows with 2.8 million.

New 1994 chip announcements already are significantly changing both device complexity levels and architectural approaches. The TI 320C80 digital signal processing device, with five separate programmable processors, has about 4.5 million transistors. Another example is the 26 million transistor Analog Devices 21060 chip. Its high transistor count arises from its large amount of memory on-board the chip. Power dissipation for current devices ranges from about 1 watt to 30 Watts. CMOS dissipation is usually dominated by dynamic power (i.e., CV^2f).

Fabrication processes developed for low voltage operation provide an important edge in achieving high throughput per watt performance. For a given voltage level, power is a function of circuit design and specific operating mode rather than an intrinsic technology characteristic, and the power variation between chips can be expected to remain large.

Single-chip microprocessor packages vary from about 168 to 504 pins. Signal pin counts will grow in the near term, but will not be a universal phenomena. Some processor designs will move high pin count signal interfaces on-chip. An important issue related to pin out is the need for multiple power and ground connections. In order to reduce series inductance, high-performance devices will move rapidly to hundreds of power system connections. A long-term expectation is that the positioning of device pads will move from the perimeter of chips to over the entire surface of the die.

Clock rates are typically 60 MHz for high-performance computers produced in volume, and some chips run as high as 200 MHz. A new version of the DEC Alpha chip fabricated with 0.5 micron technology is expected to run with a 300 MHz clock. It is now common for chips to employ on-chip clocks which are much faster than the off-chip clock. Factors of two times, three times, and four times are being used.

National Roadmap for Silicon Technology

The existence of a national roadmap for the development of semiconductor technology greatly simplifies the task of visualizing the future capabilities of CMOS devices. The Semiconductor Industries Association sponsored the development and publication of a national consensus roadmap to aid in research and development planning. The essence of the 1992 version of the roadmap is captured in Table 5.1. Unfortunately, the map does not project far enough in time to directly address the Petaflops challenge.

The roadmap presents a vision of successively reduced feature size CMOS generations extending forward at a three-year intervals. Each new generation can support memory devices of four times greater density that the previous generation. The 1992 map stopped at 0.1 micrometers

Table 5.1
National Roadmap for Semiconductor Technology (1992 Version)

Year	1995	1998	2001	2004	2007
Feature size (microns)	0.35	0.25	0.18	0.12	0.1
Gates/chip	800k	2M	5M	10M	20M
Bits/chip DRAM	64M	265M	1G	4G	16G
Bits/chip SRAM	16M	64M	256M	1G	4G
Wafer Processing Cost ($/cm)	3.90	3.80	3.70	3.60	3.50
Chip size (mm^2) logic per microprocessor	400	600	800	1000	1250
Chip size (mm^2) DRAM	200	320	500	700	1000
Wafer diameter (mm)	200	200–400	200–400	200–400	200–400
Defect Density (defects/cm^2)	0.05	0.03	0.01	0.004	0.002
Interconnect levels (logic)	4–5	5	5–6	6	6–7
Max power (W/die) high performance	15	30	40	40–120	40–200
Max power (W/die) portable	4	4	4	4	4
Power supply (V) desktop	3.3	2.2	2.2	1.5	1.5
Power supply (V) portable	2.2	2.2	1.5	1.5	1.5
Number of I/Os	750	1500	2000	3500	5000
Performance (MHz) off-chip	100	175	250	350	500
Performance (MHz) on-chip	200	350	500	700	1000

because reduced insulator thickness was expected to result in undesired conduction mechanisms such as tunneling, and also that subthreshold leakage would restrict device options. It seemed that a paradigm shift to quantum mechanical devices was likely: that the historic CMOS progression would finally end.

Since the 1992 roadmap was prepared, however, additional learning has taken place. Expectations now are that more or less conventional CMOS technology generations will continue until at least the 0.05 micrometer level, and perhaps as small as the 0.025 micrometer level. Also, power dissipation is expected to receive a great deal of development attention, and that the dissipation of even very high-performance chips will be modest. Because the roadmap is a living document, the Semiconductor Research Corporation is hosting planning sessions to revisit the predictions with a view to maintaining a technology plan that is updated every few years, and always extends forward about 15 years. A revised roadmap is expected to be issued in November, 1994.

Projected Year 2015 Devices

Can CMOS technology meet the needs of Petaflops computing machines? This question was examined by projecting the capability of a typical 1994 processor to very small feature size devices. This exploratory exercise led to the conclusion that a year 2015 device based on 0.05 micrometer technology could be a reasonable building block for a Petaflops system. Table 5.2 summarizes the results of the working group's "extrapolations" three generations forward from the current roadmap, from 2007 to 2015.

The tabulated technology parameters are a simple extension of the published technology roadmap together with the assumption that all three device generations will use 0.9 volt supply voltage. The present heavy development focus on portable equipment assures that low voltage processes and low power circuit techniques will emerge for even high-performance circuits. It is likely that advanced microprocessors will contain a large amount of memory on-board the chip.

Power density (Watts/unit area) in the memory regions of each chip was assumed to be lower than in the processing logic regions, because a substantially smaller proportion of the transistors are switching at a time. Also, it was assumed that memory power increased by a factor of only 1.4 when the memory capacity doubled.

Table 5.2
CMOS Technology and Parallel Processor Chip Projections

	Technology Roadmap Year	2007	2010	2013
	Device Introduction Year	2009	2012	2015
Technology Characteristics	feature size (microns)	0.1	0.07	0.05
	voltage level	0.9	0.9	0.9
	clock (MHz)	1000	1400	2000
Processor Chip with 1 MByte Memory per Node	peak throughput (Gflops)	128	360	1024
	chip power (Watts)	28	54	110
	chip memory (MBytes)	64	128	256
	number of nodes	64	128	256
Processor Chip with 8 MBytes Memory per Node	peak throughput (Gflops)	32	90	256
	chip power (Watts)	22	44	89
	chip memory (MBytes)	128	256	512
	number of nodes	16	32	64
Processor Chip with 16 MBytes Memory/Node	peak throughput (Gflops)	16	45	128
	chip power (Watts)	20	39	80
	chip memory (MBytes)	128	256	512
	number of nodes	8	16	32

The most difficult aspect of device scaling is expected to be management of the on-chip interconnect. If device dimensions are to scale in accord with the minimum feature size, the number of layers of interconnect must grow and the pitch between interconnect lines must shrink to accomplish the improved density. It is unlikely that a simple continuation of present day interconnect practices will accomplish the necessary improvement. At the very least, hierarchical levels of interconnect are anticipated, and it is likely that some portion of the interconnect function will be performed in an off-chip substrate.

No sophisticated device architectural innovations are assumed in predicting device throughput. The assumption is that two instructions will be executed per clock period. (This, however, is a very pessimistic assumption. At these small feature sizes, the area penalty for using very elaborate node architectures is nil, and the trend most probably will be to increase greatly the instructions per clock period.) The only architectural matters touched on are the amount of memory per node and the number of nodes per chip. The arbitrary memory sizes of one Megabyte per node and eight Megabytes per node were chosen to illustrate the general nature of the memory sizing trade-off. The two issues of concern are the bandwidth of the processing node to memory connection, and the device and system level power dissipation.

In addition to the processor chips discussed above, a Petaflops machine will require memory devices. In view of the historical record, there is no rationale for assuming anything other than that the density progression expressed in the 1992 roadmap will continue through the 0.05 micrometer generation. At 0.1 micrometers, the roadmap predicted 16 Gigabyte DRAMs. Using the rule of thumb of a four times density increase per generation leads to a prediction of 256 Gigabyte devices at 0.05 micrometers. Achieving this density seems impossible from the perspective of the current state of the art, but such has been the case for all past projections of electronic device capabilities two decades into the future.

Another speculation is that it will be necessary to build SRAM parts rather than DRAM because of subthreshold leakage concerns. If that is the case, the density should be predicted to be one-fourth of the DRAM value, or 64 Gigabytes.

To be useful for Petaflops applications, the memory device architectures must be revised to provide very high I/O bandwidth. Wide words will be the norm. The chips will have area array connections to support both a large number of signal lines as well as distribution of power and ground to local regions on the chip.

Technology Suitability for Petaflops Computer

To achieve a viable component count for a Petaflops computer, the building block processor chip must provide about 100 Gigaflops peak performance. Using circuit architectures comparable to those of today's devices, only two to four Gigaflops per processor node are predictable based on growth of fabrication technology speed capability. In other words, viable chip designs should contain 32 or more nodes, where each node comprises a processor, dedicated buffer memory and ancillary interface logic.

To sustain continuous computation each node must have high-speed access to memory to obtain instructions and data. A design decision must be made as to how much memory should be placed on the processor chip with each node, and how much off-chip memory needs to be available for high-speed access by the multinode chip. The traditional approach has been to use off-chip memory as the primary memory resource, and limit on-chip memory to registers and small amounts of critical cache.

For a given target chip area (based on fabrication economics), the addition of node memory reduces the number of nodes per chip and increases the power per node. On-chip memory requires much less power than the equivalent amount of off-chip power, so the net system power is probably reduced as on-chip memory increases. If only small amounts of memory are included on-chip, it is likely that at least one memory chip will be required for each processor chip.

The problem of processing node-to-memory communication is a central machine design issue. With multi-Gigahertz clock rates, the processor-to-off-chip memory interface is a difficult problem. Ideally, every on-chip node should have a wide bandwidth connection directly to the off-chip memory resources. Even with flip-chip area array devices, the physical limitations of pin count, electrical connection paths, and power dissipation make this arrangement very difficult. The off-chip memory is forced to be a shared resource, and it is probably be a limiting factor for throughput.

Use of on-chip memory eases the processing-node-to-memory interface problems. Pin count limitations are eased, and wide communication buses are practical. Shorter processor-to-memory connection lengths result in reduced line loading, smaller drivers, and less power dissipation. Because the memory and processor are designed at the same time, the detailed architecture, timing, and control of the memory can be tailored to meet the needs of the processor. In general, higher performance is achievable. To illustrate some of the general features of a potential 0.05 micrometer technology, CMOS-based Petaflops computer, a few parameters are tabulated in Table 5.3.

Processor chip count, power consumption, and on-chip memory are listed. Each row corresponds to the chip classes presented in the previous processor chip projection table. For example, the last row in the table is based on a 0.05 micrometer technology, 16 Megabyte per node, 32-node chip. For these architectural variations, the processor chip count varies from about 1,000 to 8,000. The power varies from about 100 kilowatts to over 600 kilowatts. When the need for external memory chips is included, the power could easily double. Use of lower on-chip memory devices such as the one Megabyte per node option will reduce the processor chip count

Table 5.3
Processor Chip Requirements for a Petaflops Machine Using 0.05 Micron Technology

Chip Gflops	Chip MBytes	Chip Watts	Number of chips	Power kwatts	Memory GBytes
1024	256	110	977	107	250
256	512	89	3906	348	2000
128	512	80	7813	625	4000

(i.e., the same node count but more nodes per chip), and will increase the requirement for off-chip memory.

In light of what has been achieved manufacturing supercomputers in the past, none of these parameters pose unmanageable problems. In fact, the assumption of no throughput improvement derived from architectural innovations makes these predictions overly conservative. If devices of this density and level of performance can be produced, the implementation of a Petaflops processor becomes largely an engineering problem. The physical structure and thermal management issues are similar to those associated with past supercomputer designs. The electrical interconnect and clock distribution at Gigahertz rates will be difficult, but solutions can be achieved.

Problems requiring some research and development will be the distribution of a 0.9 volt supply and ground, and the management of switching noise. For the 0.05 micron generation it appears that Petaflops machine construction will be viable with considerable margin. For the 0.1 and 0.07 micrometer generations, architectural features probably can be introduced to provide enhanced node throughput. If that proves to be true, the building block performance will be significantly enhanced and Petaflops machines can be introduced many years earlier.

5.3 Optical Devices

Interconnects, memory, and processors constitute the three main sectors of any computing system. The potential impact of optics on each of these sectors is described in this section.

Interconnects

Due to the uncharged nature of photons, optical interconnections potentially offer freedom from mutual coupling effects. This characteristic greatly differentiates optical interconnections from electrical ones based on charged carriers (i.e., electrons). Because the capacitive coupling between electrical interconnects increases with increasing signal frequency, the advantage of optical interconnects becomes more important as the need for interconnect bandwidth increases. Although advanced dielectrics can overcome the electrical coupling effects at the lower frequencies, at frequencies approaching the GHz range the frequency dependence of known dielectrics leads to severe limitations for electrical interconnects at the bandwidths that will be required for Petaflops computers.

The uncharged nature of photons leads to another advantage for optical interconnects in Petaflops computers: lower power consumption for the longer interconnects. With electrical interconnects the charge of the electrons leads to a distributed capacitance along the interconnects. Consequently, to accompany the resistivity of metallic conductors, electrical interconnects have an energy requirement that increases with increasing interconnect length. But, for optical interconnects, the energy requirement lies with the optical source and the optical detector rather than distributed along the interconnect. Therefore, beyond some distance (dependent on many link parameters), the optical interconnect becomes more energy efficient. Since this break-even distance can be as small as subcentimeter, optical interconnects can lead to a considerable energy savings for large computing systems such as Petaflops computers, that likely will have hundreds of thousands of interconnects longer than a centimeter (or whatever the break-even distance is).

Optical interconnects have numerous other advantages that may be important to Petaflops computing, such as the ability to frequency multiplex optical signals, electrical isolation between optically interconnected electronic circuits, increased fan-out capability (due to a freedom from capacitive loading effects), and a greater flexibility of routing because optical beams can pass through one another, and the freedom from routing signals in the presence of ground planes. But, the advantages of larger bandwidths and lower energy requirements for the longer interconnects are the most important reasons for optics in Petaflops computing sys-

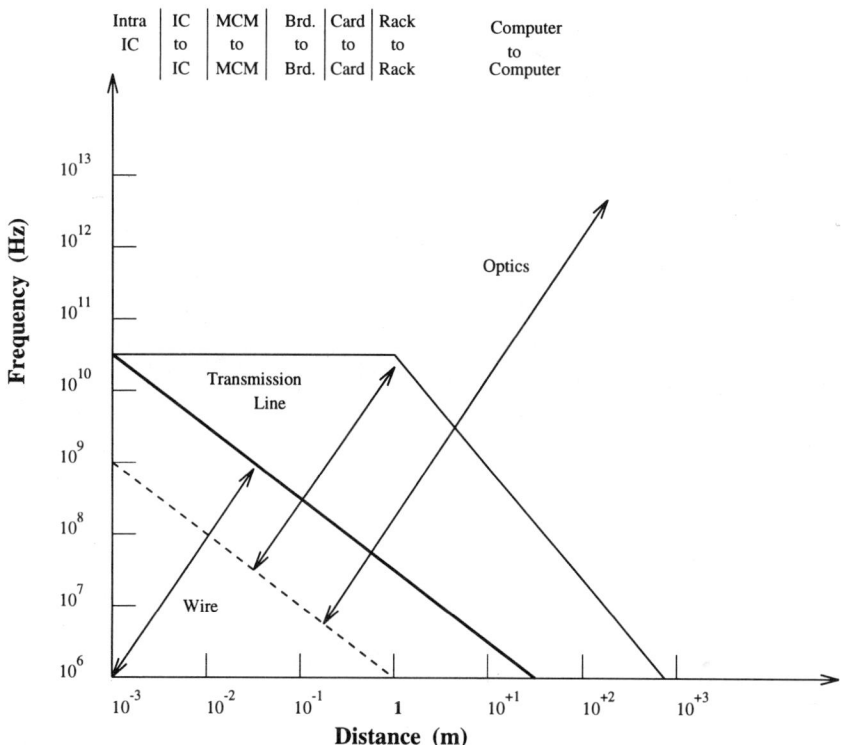

Figure 5.1
Optics: The preferred interconnect technology for the higher frequency and longer distance applications [Feldman:88a], [Tsang:90a].

tems. Figure 5.1 illustrates the frequency (bandwidth) and distance limitations of electrical interconnects. It clearly shows that the 10–100 GHz clock speeds projected for Petaflops systems will require these systems to be heavily dependent on optical interconnects.

Optical interconnects may be divided into two classes: guided (fibers and waveguides) and free-space. Since each class has a very different application within Petaflops systems, they will be addressed separately.

Guided Optical Interconnects Fibers and waveguides function as the "wires" for optical interconnects, with fibers being similar to copper wires and waveguides similar to microstrips and striplines. Commercially available fiber optic networks are now being used for computer-to-computer interconnects and computer-to-peripheral connections. As the need grows for higher performance systems, guided optical interconnects will start to see use within the computer, possibly as far down into the packaging hierarchy as MCM-to-MCM (multichip module, or wafer-to-wafer).

Electrical interconnects achieve some bandwidth enhancement through time division multiplexing (TDM) and spatial multiplexing (e.g., ribbon cables). But the immense bandwidth available in optical waveguides ($\approx$THz) has opened up additional avenues to bandwidth enhancement for optical interconnects, namely, wavelength division multiplexing (WDM) and subcarrier multiplexing (SCM). This added capability could be critical for Petaflops systems due to parallelism requirements that could exceed one million channels. Novel schemes for combining spatial multiplexing with TDM, WDM, and SCM for optical interconnection may be needed.

Free-Space Interconnects Guided optical interconnects suffer from one of the disadvantages of electrical interconnects, that is, the need for a physical guiding medium. This leads to several serious packaging limitations in applications (e.g., Petaflops computers) requiring a large number of interconnections. First, only one physical guide can occupy a given position in space, and second, attaching a large number of guides to an optoelectronic component is difficult and costly. Free-space optical interconnects, however, do not require a "guide"; therefore, a large degree of spatial multiplexing is possible. For example, a 100 × 100 array of vertical-cavity surface-emitting lasers (VCSELs) could be used to transmit 10,000 signals simultaneously to an array of photodiodes in any specified pattern. This can be done far more compactly than through 10,000 fibers.

The value of free-space interconnection in the Petaflops environment can be appreciated by considering two of the architectural scenarios that have been proposed for such systems. For the scenario of ten thousand 100-Gigaflops CPUs, on the order of 100 billion memory accesses per second will be required. Assuming a 64-bit word, this implies a 6,400 Gigabytes/sec transfer rate between processor and memory, requiring 64 100-Gigabytes/sec optical interconnects. In addition, assuming one of 10 CPU instructions is I/O with a peripheral (implying a 640 Gigabytes/sec transfer rate), seven 100-Gigabytes/sec fibers would be required. Finally, assuming one of 100 CPU instructions involves communicating with another processor (implying a 64 Gigabytes/sec transfer rate), an additional 100-Gigabytes/sec link would be required.

If the computer is packaged as 10 MCMs per board, 10 boards per card cage, and 10 card cages per rack, then assuming a factor of 10 increase in connectivity from rack-to-card cage-to-board-to-MCM, 64 100-Gigabytes/sec connections between processor and memory (rack-to-rack) implies 640 10-Gigabytes/sec links between card cages, and 6,400 one-Gigabyte/sec links between boards, and 64,000 100-Megabytes/sec connections between MCMs. Since there are 10,000 CPUs (1 CPU/MCM), the figures translate into $(64 + 7 + 1) \times 10,000 = 720,000$ 100-Gigabytes/sec optical links and $640 \times 10,000 = 6,400,000$ 10-Gigabytes/sec optical links, a packaging and manufacturing nightmare. For the architectural scenario of 100,000 10-Gigaflops CPUs, the above reasoning leads to a requirement for 800,120 100-Gigabytes/sec links and 7,000,000 10-Gigabytes/sec links. Free-space implementation does not need a physical guiding medium for each individual beam, thereby greatly simplifying the problems in attempting to interconnect such computing systems.

Free-space interconnects have the additional advantage of being reconfigurable en-mass by modifying a beam steering element (e.g., a diffraction grating or hologram) in the media through which the interconnect beams pass. This could lead to special-purpose machines becoming more general purpose, and to computing systems enhancing performance by selecting the interconnection structure most appropriate for the task at hand at any instant of time.

Memory

The past 10 years have seen the optical storage business go from non-existent to a rapidly growing business offering a diversity of products with enhanced storage capacities, such as disks (128 Megabytes to 20 Gigabytes), tape (50 Gigabytes to 1 Terabyte), and card (4 Megabytes). Two of the major attractions of optical storage systems are their ability to store large amounts of information in a reasonably small volume and their long storage times (> 10 years). Although the existing media are planar, there is considerable research into three-dimensional (and even four-dimensional) optical storage systems. These will be treated separately for the purposes of this technology introduction.

Planar Optical Storage Of the planar optical storage techniques, the one most appropriate for Petaflops systems is the optical disk technology with a potential capacity approaching 100 Gigabits and a data transfer rate as high as 10 Megabytes per second; however, like magnetic disk technology, it suffers from a relatively slow access time (milliseconds), due to the reliance on mechanical motion. Although there has been research into optoelectronic and acousto-optic scanning of planar media, the systems continue to consist of a rotating medium being addressed by a single optical head.

Because Petaflops systems will require large throughput of data, optical disk systems must increase the readout data rate. This may be accomplished by employing parallel readout, a solution whose time has probably arrived. If the bits to be read out in parallel are stored adjacent to one another in some rectangular or circular area, a single laser beam can be used to illuminate this area, and the bits can be read out in parallel via a two-dimensional photodetector array. If the bits can not be stored in such a regular pattern, the optical addressing may be accomplished by using a free-space interconnect system as was described above.

3-D Optical Storage Three-dimensional storage, a phenomena which has eluded systems, uses electrical interconnects to address the storage locations, such as conventional electronic and magnetic memories. Due to the uncharged nature of photons, light beams can pass through a 3-D transparent storage media to address any site in the storage volume. Although individual sites can be addressed in some of the 3-D systems, the tremendous capacity (thousands of Petabits or more) leads to page addressing. Although the access time for locating a page may be relatively slow (microseconds or more), the readout data rates have the potential to be exceptionally fast (Megabits per nanosecond).

Numerous 3-D storage systems have been proposed, but those appearing to receive the most attention are: holostore based on photorefractive rods (potential capacity of a Terabit and data transfer rate of 10 Terabits per second) [Parish:90a], two-photon 3-D memory (potential capacity of 0.1 Petabit and data transfer rate of a Terabit per second) [Hunter:90a], and spectral hole burning. Larger capacities than a Terabit have been proposed for holographic storage by combining it with spectral hole burning (4-D memory) to achieve capacities of a Petabit, but the high risk of such a storage concept at the present time resulted in the working group not considering to propose this for a Petaflops program.

Processors

It seems reasonable to assume that for the foreseeable future, the electronic transistor will be superior to its optical equivalent in terms of size, ease of VLSI integration, and power consumption. Given this assumption, the working group believes it is reasonable to assume that the CPUs of computers will remain electronic for some time. At the same time, because of the high bandwidth achievable in optical devices, it seems reasonable to assume that they will be used in simple and regular architectures. These include neural networks and communications-intensive applications, such as data communications switching in which optical switching could avoid a massive number of photon/electron conversions. Therefore, optical switching might have some role to play in Petaflops computers, e.g., controlling high-speed networks, but will not likely be used for the central processors.

5.4 Projections for Technology Development

Optical interconnects and optical memory are both relatively immature technologies, having reached the marketplace with initial products just within the past decade. But both are rapidly emerging, with many envisioned products in sight. As discussed above, some of these are strong candidates for realizing a Petaflops computing capability. The three tables that follow reflect the working group's projections about the extent the technologies will continue to emerge over the next 20 years. These projections provide a basis for hardware decisions in planning the development of Petaflops systems.

Tables 5.4 and 5.5 address optical interconnects, dividing them into guided interconnects and free-space interconnects. This division is necessary since the application of these two types of optical interconnects in Petaflops computers is quite different; while the guided interconnects will function mostly as point-to-point interconnects, the free-space inter-

Table 5.4
Projections for development of optical guided wave technologies for optical interconnection.

Emerging Capabilities for Guided Optical Interconnects

	Example	Speed	Power	Technology
Current Capability	HP and AT&T SONET	100 Mb/s 2.5 Gb/s	1–2 Watts 10 Watts	LED* LD*
10-Year Projection		100 Gb/s	1 Watt	LD (WDM or TDM)*
20-Year Projection		1 Tb/s	10 Watts	LD (WDM and TDM)

*LED (Light Emitting Diode), LD (Laser Diode), WDM (Wavelength Division Multiplexing), TDM (Time Division Multiplexing)

Table 5.5
Projections for development of optical free-space technologies for optical interconnection.

Emerging Capabilities for Free-Space Optical Interconnects

	Example	Perf.	Speed/Channel	Power	Technology
Current Capability	AT&T Switching Fabric	0.15 Tb/s	150 MB/s	10 Watts	S-SEED*
10-Year Projection		1 Petabit/s	10 Gb/s	100 Watts	FED-SEED MQW Mode VCSEL*
20-Year Projection		10 Petabits/s	10 Gb/s	1 KW	VCSEL Smart Pixels

*S-SEED (Symmetric Self Electrooptic Effect Device),
FET-SEED (Field Effect Transistor Self Electrooptic Effect Device),
MQW Mod. (Multiple Quantum Well Modulators),
VCSEL (Vertical-Cavity Surface-Emitting Laser Diodes).

connects will function as broadcast and random interconnects. The first line of each table provides baseline information by giving an example of where the technology is now. Table 5.6 addresses optics for memory. The largest impediment to the introduction of optical interconnects is cost. It is expected that optical interconnects will continue to ride the learning curve in terms of costs.

Table 5.6
Projections for development of optics for memory.

Emerging Capabilities for Optical Memory

	Example	Memory Size	Access Speed	Transfer Rate	Technology
Current Capability	CD ROMs	600 Mbytes	10 millisec.	3 Mbits/sec.	Optical Disk
10-Year Projection		0.1 Petabit	1 microsec.	10^{15} bits/sec.	Two-Photon Medium Holographic with SHB* Acousto-optic Scanners
20-Year Projection		100 Petabits	0.1 microsec.	10^{15} bits/sec.	Two-Photon 2-D SLM Addressed* Database Filters

*SHB (Spectral Hole Burning), SLM (Spatial Light Modulator).

5.5 Optical Technology Mapped onto Proposed Petaflops Scenarios

Three scenarios for constructing a Petaflops computer were presented by the Architecture Working Group. The first was a network of supercomputers (e.g., vector based, low latency architecture), the second was a massively parallel system composed of a network of high-performance workstations (e.g., Intel Paragon), and the third was a fine-grain, active memory machine. From the standpoint of establishing interconnect and memory requirements, these three architectures can be summarized in terms of their degree of parallelism and their grain size in the following manner:

10^4 100 Gigaflops processor nodes

10^5 10 Gigaflops processor nodes

10^6 1 Gigaflops processor nodes

Interconnects For the purpose of matching the capabilities of optical interconnects with the projected needs of the three proposed architectures, the working group divided each architecture into a plausible packaging hierarchy of integrated circuits (ICs), MCMs (or wafers), boards, card cages, and racks. This is equivalent to dividing the problem into levels of flops that must be processed. For example, for scenario 3, an IC is likely to accommodate 10 CPUs for a total processing capability of 10 Gigaflops, an MCM would be about 10 ICs, resulting in 100 Gigaflops, etc. Moving up to scenario 2, each IC would likely be a CPU, thus having the same 10 Gigaflops capacity as was the case at the IC level for scenario 3. The packaging hierarchy that the working group used is illustrated in Table 5.7, which lists the most promising optical interconnect methodologies recommended by the working group for each level of the packaging hierarchy and for each of the three scenarios. The need for free-space optics at the IC-to-IC and MCM-to-MCM levels will vary depending on the degree of coupling that is desired. For example, for scenario 3, the sheer magnitude of the interconnecting network needed to provide a high degree of coupling among the one million processors may necessitate free-space optics.

Note that free-space optics is shown as impacting the processor level of scenario 1 (where multiple ICs will be needed for each CPU) even

Table 5.7
Places within Petaflops computer hierarchy where various optical interconnect technologies will likely be needed. This is shown for each of the three proposed Petaflops architectures.

Optical Interconnects for Petaflops Computers

	IC-to-IC (10 GF)	MCM-to-MCM (100 GF)	Inter-Board (1 TF)	Inter-Card Cage (10 TF)	Inter-Rack (100 TF)
10^4 100 GF CPUs	Free-Space	Guided Free-Space 1 CPU	Fiber Free-Space 10 CPUs	Fiber Ribbon Fiber WDM* Optical MIN* 100 CPUs	Fiber Ribbon Fiber WDM Fiber TDM* 100 GHz Fbr. 1000 CPUs
10^5 10 GF CPUs	Free-Space 1 CPU	10 CPUs	Optical MIN Opt. LAN* 100 CPUs	Full Connectivity 100 GHz Fbr. 1000 CPUs	Opt. LAN Optical Crossbar 10,000 CPUs
10^6 1 GF CPUs	Free-Space 10 CPUs	Free-Space 100 CPUs	Free-Space 1000 CPUs	Full Connectivity 100 GHz Fbr. 10,000 CPUs	Opt. LAN Optical Crossbar 100,000 CPUs

*WDM (Wavelength Division Multiplexing), MIN (Multistage Interconnection) Network), TDM (Time Division Multiplexing), LAN (Local Area Network)

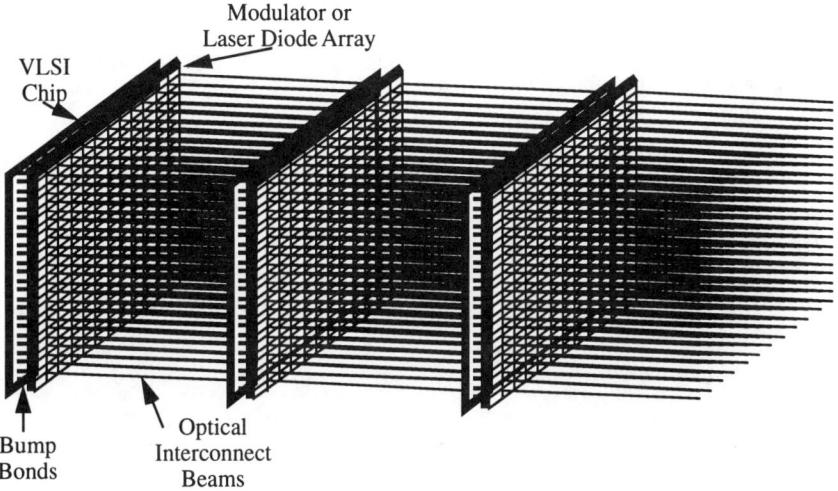

Figure 5.2
Three-dimensional Packaging of VLSI Chips using Optical Interconnection.

though it was stated earlier that optics had little foreseeable impact for processors. Free-space optics was included here after receiving the report of the semiconductor working group that noted the probable avenue to 100-Gigaflops processors was via three-dimensional stacks of chips with interchip optical interconnects. It is within the reach of today's technology for a chip 10 mm on a side to be bump bonded to a 100×100 optical modulator or laser diode array, providing 10,000 pinouts between adjacent chips in a stack as illustrated in Figure 5.2. It is projected that within 10 years, the number of optical pinouts could increase by at least an order-of-magnitude. Although optics is an integral part of such a processor, its function is really interconnection rather than processing.

Memory Table 5.8 is the optical memory counterpart to Table 5.7, which was for optical interconnects. It will not be a technological challenge to provide sufficient memory capacity for Petaflops systems, but research is needed to improve access times for optical memories. With respect to CD ROMs, this may be accomplished by employing multiple read-heads placed strategically around the disk. No matter what the storage technology, increased access time goes along with increased capacity. But the advantage of optical memory is that it lends itself well

Table 5.8
Places within the Petaflops computer hierarchy where various optical memory technologies will likely be needed. This is shown for each of the three proposed Petaflops architectures.

Optical Memory for Petaflops Computers

	Cache	RAM	Disk	Archival
10^4 100 GF CPUs	Optically Interconnected 3D Memory Electronic RAM	LD Arrays*	CM ROM with Optical Tape	CD ROM
10^5 10 GF CPUs	Optically Interconnected Electronic RAM	3D Memory	RAIDs* (CD ROM)	CD ROM Optical Tape
10^6 1 GF CPUs	Optically Interconnected Electronic RAM	3D Memory	RAIDs (CD ROM)	CD ROM Optical Tape

*ROM (Read Only Memory), LD (Laser Diode), RAIDs (Redundant Arrays of Independent Disks)

to parallel addressing due to the ability to image data from the memory; therefore, once the desired data field has been accessed, the data readout rates can be extremely high. This implies that optical memories may be well suited to Petaflops computers designed to work with large two-dimensional data fields, such as images and other multidimensional signals.

Table 5.8 indicates places within the Petaflops computer hierarchy where various optical memory technologies will likely be needed for each of the three proposed Petaflops architectures.

Device Technology Working Group: 97

Table 5.9
Recommended research programs to support the insertion of optics technology into Petaflops computing systems.

Research Areas Needing Support	Recommended Support ($M)
Smart pixel arrays	80
Interconnection optical	60
Optical memory backplane	40
3D memory addressing	50
Interface to Josephson Junction CPUs	40
Optical I/O for ICs	80
Optical CAD tools	50
All-optical Terahertz logic	40
Optical radio	40

5.6 Future R&D in Optics

A considerable amount of research and development remains to be done to reach the projected performance levels listed above for the optics technologies. Listed in Table 5.9 are the recommendations of the committee on research directions that need to be pursued in support of any national thrust to develop Petaflops computing systems. The dollar amounts associated with each recommendation are rough estimates of the investment needed over the next 10 years to ensure timely insertion of the technologies. The first two items, smart pixel arrays and interconnection optics, are already receiving some support, but the recommendation is to expand the support in these areas. The remaining entries in Table 5.9 are recommended research programs to support the insertion of optics technology into Petaflops computing systems.

A brief discussion of each of the recommended research areas follows:

Smart Pixel Arrays provide the interface between parallel electronics and parallel optics in that each element (pixel) of the array has both electrical and optical inputs and both electrical and optical outputs, and they provide a localized processing capability at each pixel. These arrays will be critical for the realization of large-scale parallelism for optical interconnection and optical memory addressing. Research is needed in integrating the electronics and optics, improving thermal management, and providing adequate interfaces to the arrays.

Interconnection Optics includes conventional optics needed in the guided or free-space channels. Research is needed to miniaturize light shaping and directing elements (e.g., lenses and computer-generated holograms), to realize single-mode fiber arrays, and to create an optical "HIPPI" standard for 100-Gigabytes/sec links.

Optical Memory Backplane calls for the development of optical interconnections between memory boards for the purpose of realizing required fanouts in memory addressing. As mentioned previously, optical interconnection avoids the capacitive loading problems associated with fanouts in electrically interconnected systems that cause an increase in the RC time constant. In addition, the outputs of the memory chips have to be ORed together, creating quite a load on the drivers of these chips, thus slowing them down. Optical ORing would be faster.

3-D Memory Addressing needs research to search for efficient ways to store and read out such large data stores, and to develop the required technologies for rapidly focusing the addressing beams to the desired spots within the 3-D storage media.

Interface to Josephson Junction CPUs calls for research to develop optical links that can provide interconnections with the outside world for processors inside the cryogenic environment. The problem with electrical connections for this application is that they conduct heat into the cryogenic chambers.

Optical I/O for ICs is intended to address the packaging issues related to providing ICs with optical interconnects, and to support a competition between the electronic and the optical communities to determine the demonstrated limits to how many I/O pins can be achieved on ICs by electrical and optical interconnects, respectively.

Optical CAD Tools are the optical counterpart to the electronic CAD tools that have been so successful in enabling system designers to work with complex systems. Research is needed not only to develop needed tools, but to integrate all of the available tools into a user-friendly CAD system for optoelectronic design.

All-Optical Terahertz Logic will be needed for high-speed controllers for switched optical links (e.g., the optical crossbar), for high-speed interface units needed to load and unload data to and from high-performance fiber networks, and to implement multiplexers and demultiplexers needed for TDM fiber networks.

Optical Radio is an interesting concept that should be researched as a way of providing general interest data throughout Petaflops systems (e.g., for distribution of instructions or maintenance of cache coherency). Many different optical signals are broadcast simultaneously to many different receivers which choose which signals to "listen to" at any particular time.

5.7 Superconductive Electronics for Petaflops Computing

Superconductivity offers unique and quite important performance features to future supercomputing systems. The logic gates operate with picosecond (10^{-12} sec) delays while dissipating microwatts of power. Second, since the conductors have zero resistance at DC and very low loss at multi-Gigahertz frequencies, it is possible to exploit very wideband, impedance-matched transmission lines (a) on-chip, (b) between chips and (c) between multichip modules (MCMs). In combination, these features enable the construction of a supercomputer processor with a multi-Gigahertz clock rate. The very low power consumption allows it to have a very small size, greatly alleviating the "time-of-flight" problem inherent in multi-Gigahertz clock systems. The device technology and the other necessary building blocks are sufficiently advanced today that a program to integrate them into a demonstration system should be established. The essential hardware ingredients required to assemble a machine based upon superconductivity are logic, memory, and interconnect.

Logic

Numerous workers in Japan and the U.S. have demonstrated circuit performance with picosecond delays at the microwatt per gate power level. In addition, VLSI level *chips* have been built and tested that show the same fundamental performance. These demonstrations included on-chip RAM and ROM to maintain properly the level of functionality needed at one GHz clock rates. The obvious conclusion is that circuit and manufacturing margins can be achieved at VLSI levels of integration, albeit not at the density presently available in *mature* silicon technology.

Memory

Demonstrations of memory chip performance in purely superconductive devices have not been as impressive in density per chip; nevertheless, they have repeated the speed and power features of the logic circuits. The level of research and development effort has been much smaller than that applied to logic circuits. Thus, although only a 4K RAM at 500 picosecond access time has been demonstrated successfully in Japan, layouts have been made for 64 K RAM chips expected to have 500 picosecond access time, and recently, 16 K sections were built and are under testing. Given the present all-superconductive circuits and what is currently known, it is generally believed that the best path to follow to achieve large memory chips at low power is to implement hybrids: superconductor-semiconductor circuits. It is also expected that proper use of cryogenic CMOS will assist in solving the speed/size requirements. Nevertheless, it is feasible to build purely superconductive ROM and RAM at levels of integration appropriate to "buffering" the processor requests.

Interconnects

On-chip Circuits on a superconductive chip are basically low impedance. The connections between these, of necessity and naturally, are made with superconducting transmission lines. Since the lines involve "zero resistance" metallurgy, they have very low dispersion and very low loss. Therefore, routing around the chip is constrained fundamentally by time-of-flight rather than signal attenuation. (This zero resistance also can be used as interconnect on semiconductor chips to reduce the interconnect loss of submicron circuitry.)

Chip-to-Chip Multichip modules of high packing density and with multi-Gigahertz bandwidth are mandatory to transfer the on-chip circuit speed to the system level. Since the circuits are low impedance, the VLSI chip and the multichip system call for high currents. Because the power lines can be made of zero resistance buses, the voltage drop and cryogenic power supply waste can be made very small. On the MCM, the signals themselves can once again be transferred by superconductive transmission lines. It always will be necessary to have multiple levels of wiring for a multichip system, and this is achieved by alternate layers of ground and connection lines which are spaced to form strip-line or microstrip transmission lines. These low impedance lines have exceptionally low crosstalk, enhanced by the magnetic field expulsion inherent in superconductivity. Such MCMs have already been built at three levels of metallization and are now being fabricated at five levels for a 20-chip superconductive crossbar.

An alternative approach has been demonstrated by KYOCERA in conjunction with MITI's Electro-Technical Laboratory (ETL). They have built a multilevel ceramic MCM with nine levels of tungsten connectors for powering and three levels of superconductor for signal transport. The "breakthroughs" here were the ability to make a ceramic that matched the thermal expansion of the superconductive chips and the fabrication of superconductive lines on this medium. The MCM is designed to mount ETL's 4-chip prototype supercomputer and drive it at 1.25 GHz, 3.75 GHz, and finally, at 10 GHz clock rates.

MCM-to-Room Temperature Connection A cryogenic system always will have signal and power connections to room temperature. The data bandwidth for this interface will translate into hundreds of communications lines, each at Gigahertz bandwidth. For latency reasons, this physical separation must be kept short; but, for heat transport reasons, should be kept long. Multi-Gigahertz bandwidth, multiconductor copper ribbon transmission line cables with acceptable heat transfer to connect over a 6" path (800 picosecond delay) from room temperature to 4° Kelvin have been built and tested successfully as interconnect elements in a crossbar switch. This microstrip cable provides impedance-matched communication from the room temperature electronics to the cryogenic MCM and back to room temperature.

A system level of interconnection has been demonstrated at a preliminary stage by a recent set of measurements on a three-chip superconductive crossbar cross section which operated at a 2.5 Gigabytes/sec serial data rate from room temperature sources through the cryoelectronics and back to room temperature receivers. The full system, a 128 × 128,

2.5 Gigabytes/sec per port crossbar is being constructed for use in shared-memory computing or ATM switching applications.

MITI's Electro-Technical Laboratory has built a second digital test and demonstration system, a four-chip computer consisting of these chips:

- Register and ALU
- Sequence Control Unit
- Instruction ROM
- RAM.

MITI's four-chip computer was tested at low speed in 1991 and shown to be fully functional; its power dissipation was 6.2 milliwatts. The difficulties of powering, packaging, and interconnecting for very high speeds have been addressed by a joint ETL-KYOCERA effort to develop a ceramic substrate with multilevel wiring of both normal and superconducting metals.

In addition to the anticipated difficulty of making electrical connection to room temperature is the well-known problem of providing the 1.0 volt level required by room temperature semiconductor electronics, given the millivolt levels generated by superconductive electronics. Several solutions have been demonstrated: amplification at room temperature by Fujitsu (Japan), State University of New York, Tektronix, and TRW; cryogenic temperature amplification by Fujitsu (Japan) and TRW; nonlinear thresholding by Fujitsu (Japan) and Tektronix.

Physical Limits

Superconductive technology has the advantage of being a quantum mechanical phenomenon. Its zero resistance is derived from binding energies on the order of the thermal energy at the material's critical temperature (the temperature at which the metal becomes superconducting). This binding energy sets the highest frequency at which the electromagnetic photon will have enough energy to "break" the superconducting paired electrons. This results in frequency "limitations" to below a Terahertz, or subpicosecond rise time. The power limitation of the devices is set fundamentally by the requirement to store enough energy to exceed adequately thermal noise at the operating temperature (always below its critical temperature). The specific circuit/gate configurations are normally separated into those that switch between a zero voltage state and a voltage state (millivolt level), and those that store and transfer single flux quanta. The first category of circuits have been well developed; the second set are less well established. The second type offers approximately one-tenth the power consumption and higher speed operation.

The limitations imposed upon circuit density are those experienced by not-yet commercial technologies: insufficient acceptance and therefore a narrow set of practitioners. The technology is practiced using the same fabrication techniques as the semiconductor industry uses with the addition of a different metallization; it is also comprised of many fewer process steps. The process presently practiced uses $2\mu m$ (approximately) lithography which is well below what is common in the semiconductor industry. Improvements in process control and the use of high-quality, available, standard fabrication tools should permit building chips in the 100,000-gate level of complexity.

For a purely superconductive memory chip, complexity is not expected to exceed the 64 K per chip level without changes in the topology of the storage element. This arises from using the flux quantum as the stored bit; the required inductance which stores the zero resistance current, so far, has not been reduced in physical size. The access time for a modest size chip ($\approx$ 64 K) is 500 picoseconds and has been evaluated to be able to reach 100–200 picoseconds. (NEC believes Megabit per chip memories can be done.)

Barriers/Obstacles

No fundamental obstacle exists to demonstrating the viability of superconducting technology in very high-speed clock rate processors. The opportunities exist to integrate the technology with very high-speed fiber optics or free-space optical links to transfer data from room temperature to the cryogenic system and back out. Optical links would preserve short path lengths while essentially eliminating the thermal conduction penalty. Closed-cycle cooling also can be improved to provide a more commercially attractive support system. There is, finally, the opportunity to develop a fast memory that will be compatible with the processor.

R&D to Overcome Barriers and Obstacles The working group conceived a long-term R&D approach with broad program goals over the next ten years. The approach is described below in terms of a five-year program and broad 10-year goals:

Five-Year Program

Logic The present fabrication capability to achieve good yield on a 20,000- to 40,000-gate chip should be improved and stabilized. The circuit family would be adopted from the Japanese.

Memory We must re-evaluate and develop sub-nanosecond memory chips. The state of the art is not as advanced as logic, principally due to a much lower level of effort. The goal is 16 Kb to 64 Kb less than 10 milliwatts per chip with a sub-nanosecond access time. Most important is the development of a cryo-CMOS memory chip. Preliminary work is taking place at a very low level to demonstrate superconducting-semiconducting on-chip hybrids. Sense amplifiers, narrow line interconnects, and enhanced speed due to the cold environment are being evaluated. In addition, one must test the performance improvement of standard CMOS and specially processed CMOS at cryogenic temperatures.

Interconnects Chip pad configurations up to 350 I/Os at 2.5 Gigabytes/sec are presently being developed (e.g., Crossbarat MCC). For impedance and crosstalk reasons, the pad configuration described by MCC for Crossbar and by MITI's Electro Technical Laboratory, namely coaxial I/Os, should be exploited. This would improve greatly the multi-Gigahertz frequency behavior of the transition between the chips and their supporting MCM.

It will be critical to establish the MCM technology for a large chip count processor. Thus, a careful test and evaluation of KYOCERA's MCM (built for the MITI/ETL supercomputer four-chip system) is needed at a 10 GHz clock rate. This also requires cooling the MCM properly.

The connections to room temperature will necessarily be at Gigahertz rates and most likely will involve transfer rates of Terabits/sec. Impedance-matched cables of short ($\approx 6''$) length of this class of performance developed for Crossbar must be improved for both thermal and bandwidth reasons. However, a very attractive technique is to use optical I/O, either by fiber optic cable or free-space interconnect. This would provide outstanding data rates and do so with negligible heat transfer.

Device Technology Working Group:

To interconnect between processors and from processors to memory, a switching fabric must be available. The present crossbar development needs to be extended in speed or size (or both), and other switches should be evaluated and developed for this purpose.

10-Year Goals

Logic Underlying this goal is the ability to reduce the power by 10 while increasing circuit speed by five. Single flux quantum logic offers both of these features. The logic gates and circuit structures need more detailed demonstrations both in simulation and in fabrication. Also needed is an evaluation of the limits of "conventional" voltage state logic; early (i.e., 1970s) circuit structures were shown to have those speed-power properties but were not explored.

The capability to fabricate with good yield will need to be improved by inserting good but standard silicon processing tools. Along with that, design and testing will be further advanced.

Memory Continual improvement of both cryo-CMOS and superconductive memories will occur, and must occur, by silicon's normal progress and by the practice of superconductive fabrication.

Interconnects The critical steps required will be the timing and substrate issues introduced by using a clock whose period corresponds to a time-of-flight of roughly 5 mm for free-space light.

The second major challenge will be the switching interconnect. The architecture and the requisite speed to provide processor-processor and processor-memory connections will require careful, intense work. The third technical improvement will require the use of optic I/Os to achieve the necessary data bandwidths. At this point, one will most likely need to exploit the already demonstrated picosecond soliton propagation of fiber optics and the also demonstrated picosecond response time of superconductive electronics. The interface of this to the room temperature world will be a challenge. As before, the separate parts, the building blocks, must be assembled into a system demonstration to understand and to prove that the technology "works."

Table 5.10
Development Milestones for Superconductive Technology for Petaflops Computing

	Milestones	
Estimated Costs	$6M/Year	$10M/Year
Performance Metrics	5-Year (Years 1–5)	10-Year (Years 6–10)
Clock Speed	10 GHz	50 GHz
Logic Gates/Processor	10^6	4×10^6
Peak Speed	50 Gigaflops	1 Teraflops
Power at Cryo Temp.	1 Watt	4 Watts
Memory	50 Gigabytes	1 Terabytes
Wall Plug Power	10 KW	10 KW

To achieve the 10-year goals for logic, memory, and interconnects, milestones for the five- and 10-year milestones against which progress can be measured are necessary. These milestones are shown in Table 5.10.

In the first five years, the development program would focus on logic, memory, packaging, interconnection to room temperature, and switching networks. In the second five years (years 6–10), the program would focus on low-power logic, improved memory, optical I/O, and improved switch networks. The key technologies for the entire 10-year program would be cryo-CMOS, CMOS, and superconductive technologies. Important directions for funded research are listed below:

- Cryogenic sub-nanosecond memory
- Optical I/O to cryo
- Low-power circuits
- Very high-density packaging
- Design techniques and tools
- Gigahertz test techniques
- High-reliability cooling.

5.8 Device Technology Summary

Despite previous technology projections, progress in device design and manufacturing has been better than expected. Given that this trend continues, semiconductor devices should continue to be essential components of high-performance computers well past the turn of the century. But, to achieve usable Petaflops computing capabilities will require considerable effort in advancing the state of the art in optical and superconductive devices, even as semiconductor capabilities improve.

The Device Technology Working Group believes that optical interconnects and optical memory not only will provide performance enhancement for Petaflops computers, but will be critical to the realization of these computing systems. The large data transfer rates needed within Petaflops computers to avoid processors sitting idle waiting for inputs dictate that high-bandwidth optical channels be used for much of the interconnection.

The working group also believes that R&D support for smart pixel arrays and interconnection optics should be enhanced, and that R&D in other optical technology areas ranging from optical memory backplane to optical radio should be initiated.

Finally, superconductive device technology offers considerable promise for very low-power, very high-speed computing elements. Developing and implementing this technology in viable Petaflops computing systems will require R&D progress in a number of critical areas, such as cryogenic subnanosecond memory, optical I/O to cryo, very high-density packaging, and high-reliability cooling, to cite only a few. The working group believes that important progress can be realized in superconductive technology over a 10-year period for relatively modest costs.

5.9 Acknowledgments

Participants:

Carl Kukkonen (Chair)	Jet Propulsion Laboratory
Doc Bedard (Co-Chair)	National Security Agency
Joe Brewer (Co-Chair)	Westinghouse Electric Corporation
John Neff (Co-Chair)	University of Colorado
Larry Bergman	Jet Propulsion Laboratory
Paul Boudreaux	National Security Agency
Alan Huang	AT&T Bell Laboratories
Sing Lee	University of California at San Diego

Konstantin Likharev	Suny Stony Brook
Steve Nelson	Cray Research, Inc.
Steven Pei	AT&T Bell Laboratories
John Peterson	Jet Propulsion Laboratory
John Przybysz	Westinghouse Electric Corporation
Coke Reed	Supercomputing Research Center
Arnold Silver	TRW
Martin Sokoloski	Science and Technology Corporation
Anil Thakoor	Jet Propulsion Laboratory
Bob Westervelt	Harvard University

6 Architecture Working Group: Architecture and Systems

Summary

The Petaflops computer is achievable at reasonable cost with technology available in about 20 years. No paradigm shift is required to make this computer: it can be made using the paradigms that exist today. This projection is based on a number of assumptions, and it brings with it a number of challenges and directions for future activity. The key underlying issues are

1. Silicon technology can satisfy the majority of the requirements if it continues at the same rate improvement over the next 20 years. However, the Semiconductor Industry of America (SIA) technology road map projects forward only through the year 2007 because at that point feature sizes are projected to be reduced to 0.1 μm; below this size, tunneling effects alter the behavior of active devices. To sustain an additional seven years of improvement in device technology will require advances currently not projected by the SIA. However, as discussed in the section on semiconductor device options, it appears that since 1992, enough has been learned to allow a rational projection beyond 2007 to at least 0.05 μm. This appears sufficient for the Petaflops machines discussed here. Consequently, device manufacturing technology and semiconductor science are important areas of investment to sustain technological advances when feature sizes fall below 0.1 μm.

2. The Petaflops machine will rely heavily on technology developed for the larger market of machines that are much less powerful than the Petaflops machine. This is a consequence of the very large parts count for the Petaflops machine, even for the projected technology of 20 years hence. To keep the price per part as small as possible, the parts must be produced in volume for a mass market. Technology and parts developed exclusively for the Petaflops market may be very expensive relative to those for the general market, and the leverage they provide must be very high to justify the premium paid for them.

3. The panel did not reach consensus on whether or not to recommend investment in manufacturing technology for the niche markets that cover Petaflops technology. The panel, however, encourages continued research in these areas to seek advances that can provide very high leverage on performance. Niche technology might turn out to

be useful, even if expensive, and may be attractive to mainstream computing also. In the latter case, high volume production of such technology for mainstream computers could reduce costs significantly for the use of such technology in Petaflops computers.

4. Memory latency and memory bandwidth are the most critical factors that constrain performance and narrow the choices of computer structures. Latency across the longest paths in a Petacomputer, when measured in machine cycles, will grow in the coming years rather than decrease. Hence, machine structures will tend to incorporate various techniques that remove or hide latency. Local memory and cache memory tend to remove or reduce latency. Pipelining and multi-threading tend to hide latency without reducing it. The latency problem will spawn highly perfected forms of the techniques mentioned here as well as new techniques better fitted to future applications and device technologies.

5. The bandwidth per memory part, if it evolves at its present rate, in 20 years will be somewhere between 10 to 1000 times too low to support Petaflops computing. However, the internal bandwidth of memory chips, that is, the bandwidth between the on-chip memory array and a multiplexor to the output pins, is much larger than the bandwidth available at the pins. Therefore, existing internal bandwidth may be within the limits required. Future directions for memory technology will seek ways to make high bandwidth available externally and to develop architectures that make effective use of the internal memory bandwidth by placing computational logic within the memory.

6. Memory requirements for a Petaflops machine are based on a basic assumption that a balanced system requires memory bandwidth of N bytes per cycle per flops for a small fixed constant N. This assumption forces total memory bandwidth to scale linearly with the Gigaflops performance of a machine. Independently, and for other reasons, a second basic assumption is that memory size in bytes scales linearly with problem size. To the extent that these assumptions are valid, they place extraordinary demands on future memory technology. Consequently, if algorithm developers for Petaflops applications successfully develop means to conserve the use of memory per Gigaflops, the demands on memory bandwidth and memory size for Petaflops

machines may be decreased significantly. This could lead to earlier deployment and lower cost than our estimates indicate.

7. The panel speculates that I/O requirements grow less than proportionally with increases in Gigaflops of performance. If so, the I/O requirements for a Petaflops machine may be significantly less than predicted by simple scaling formulas.

6.1 Metrics and Limitations

In this section, some basic notions that dictate various characteristics of architectures are examined. The section opens with a list of key metrics and some brief explanations, and closes with a statement of three important laws.

The key metrics used to characterize high-performance computers are

- Peak operation rate—the fastest achievable rate for the computer.
- Sustainable operation rate—this rate ideally is close to peak operation rate, but could be orders of magnitude below peak operation rate for problems that are ill-suited for a particular Petacomputer architecture.
- Operation latency—the delay between the time of initiation of an operation on a set of data and the time at which the results of the operation appear at the output of the operation unit.
- Average memory system latency—the delay between request for an item and the arrival of the item. Because delays may vary depending on where the item is located when requested, latency is averaged over all the possible locations with the probabilities taken into account.
- Memory chip drain time—the time required to read all locations in a memory chip and to present the data read at the external interface of the chip.
- Memory chip cost per bit—the ratio of chip cost to number of bits per chip.
- Ratio of memory latency to operation latency—This ratio expresses the balance between memory and operation units. When the ratio is high, the memory latency may be too high to maintain full utilization of the operation units. When the ratio is very low, the operation

units may saturate well before they are able to take full advantage of the memory system. At a ratio of one, one access path of a memory system can supply one operand per operation per cycle, which is a typical design point for high-performance computer systems.

- Memory capacity—the total main memory of the computer.
- Ratio of memory capacity to performance—the ratio of Gigabytes of memory to Gigaflops of performance.
- Network bisection bandwidth—the peak rate of data transfer between one half of the computer system and the other half of the computer system.
- Per processor network bandwidth—the peak rate of data transfer between one processor and all of the other processors in a system.
- Local memory bandwidth versus network bandwidth—The bandwidth for transfers between local memory and a processor or between closely coupled local memories is generally high when such transfers are carried out on high-bandwidth local interconnections. By comparison, the bandwidth for data transfers between a processor and remote regions of a computer system that are accessible only via network interconnections may be much lower.
- Machine diameter—Measured in processor cycles, this is the length of the longest path from one processor to another processor or to an addressable region of the memory system.
- Average dependence latency—the average time that one operation stalls at a dependence until the dependence is removed. This latency arises because dependences within execution streams force some operations to wait for others.
- Best case dependence latency—the minimum latency that will be incurred when a dependence forces an operation to stall.
- Recurring Cost—the replication cost of a single machine.
- Development cost—the investment cost to develop a machine through the first few copies.
- Price—The price of a machine to a customer is a function of the replication cost plus a fraction of the development cost, plus other components, including profit. When development costs are very large, to bring price down, the number of copies over which the development

costs are shared should be as large as possible. Doubling the number of copies in use may have as great an impact on price as reducing the replication cost by a factor of two, depending on the relative size of replication and development cost.

Basic Laws

1. Concurrency=latency times bandwidth.

   Assume that a processor is fed operands at the bandwidth of B operations per cycle, each of which requires an elapsed time of L cycles. That is, each cycle the processor accepts B sets of input operands and produces B outputs, and the time elapsed between a specific input and its corresponding output is L cycles. Then the internal concurrency of the processor is $C = BL$. In other words, at any given cycle, there are BL distinct computations proceeding concurrently within the processor. This formula specifies how much concurrency must exist within a processor for a specified bandwidth and latency.

   The formula also can be applied to the latency and bandwidth of a memory system. To sustain operations at maximum rate from a memory system whose bandwidth is B and whose latency is L requires $C = BL$ concurrent access streams from the memory system to the processors, and thus the memory must be able to support C concurrent operations internally.

   Corollary: If operation latency is on the order of 1 ns (10^{-9} s), the concurrency required to achieve a processing bandwidth of Petaflops (10^{15}) must be on the order 10^6. To reduce concurrency below 10,000, the operation latency must be less than 10 ps (10^{-11} s), and to reduce concurrency below 10, the operation latency must be less than 10 femtoseconds (10^{-14} s).

2. In a machine limited by the speed of light, i.e., when the machine diameter is much greater than one cycle, if bisection bandwidth is nearly the maximum possible, the average dependence latency grows at least as fast as $p^{1/3}$ where p is the number of processors. Physical constraints on packaging and layout may raise this bound to $p^{1/2}$.

   In a machine not limited by the speed of light, that is, in a machine whose diameter is a small number of cycles close to unity, or in a machine with a very small bisection bandwidth, the dependence latency can grow at a rate proportional to $\log(p)$.

3. In a system that makes use of multiprogramming of independent processes on a single processor to improve performance, memory requirements grow linearly with the degree of multiprogramming, and thus scale proportionally with performance. Parallel applications can save memory relative to multiprogramming because memory is shared. Also, as bandwidth increases in shared-memory systems, memory requirements diminish because sharing of data can replace making copies of data.

6.2 Petaflops Architectures Design Points

The Architecture/Systems Working Group conducted a design exercise to create a rough sketch of a Petaflops machine using technology assumed to be available in 2014. The exercise revealed that a Petaflops machine can be built with the projected technology of that period at a cost comparable to that of a supercomputer in 1994. The exercise also showed that a number of assumptions drive designs in particular directions. These assumptions should be examined for validity. If they do not hold for performance in the Petaflops region, then Petaflops machines may be quite different from the panel's projections.

This section starts with an outline of three designs for supercomputers 20 years from now. The designs differ because they are each suited for a different class of problem. After discussion of the designs, the section closes with a discussion of the crucial assumptions. The most critical assumptions are the scaling laws that say that memory bandwidth per Gigaflops and total memory size per Gigaflops are constant as performance in Gigaflops increases. Another important assumption is that device technology will follow historic trends for the next 20 years.

Figures 6.1, 6.2, and 6.3 depict three architectures that are attractive for Petaflops implementations in 20 years. For the purposes of the workshop, the panel assumed that all three machines would be built and that each would have a performance rating of a fraction of a Petaflops per second. Collectively, the three machines achieve a Petaflops per second over a large class of applications, but individual applications may do best on specific machines. This analysis assumes that each machine is rated at 400 Teraflops. Applications are likely to be well-suited to one or two of the machines, if not to all three of them. Because the cost of building

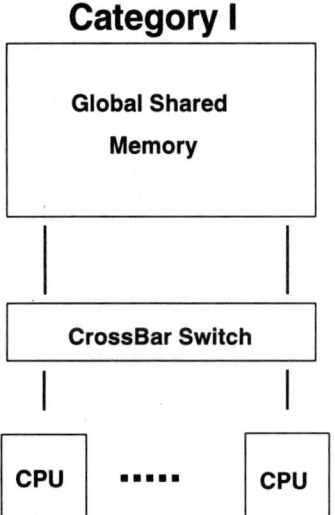

Figure 6.1
Category I architecture, global shared memory

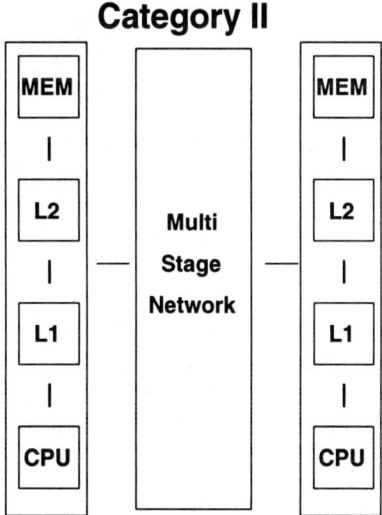

Figure 6.2
Category II architecture, network of microprocessors

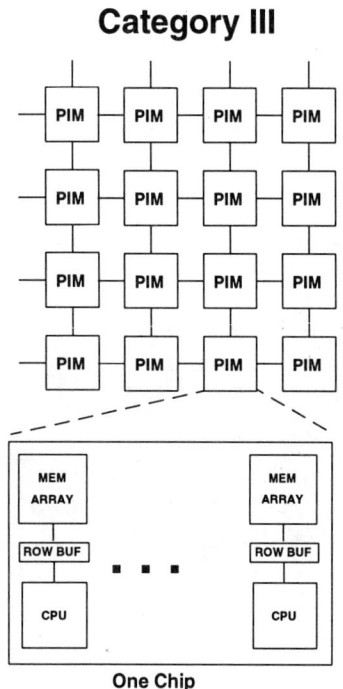

Figure 6.3
Category III architecture, processors in memory (PIM)

a 400 Teraflops machine may be less than a third of the cost of building a Petaflops machine, the panel expects that all three of the machines can be built for the cost of building a single Petaflops machine, and that the three machines can achieve an aggregate of a Petaflops performance over a much broader range of applications than can a single Petaflops machine.

The machines architectures are

- *Category 1:* Shared memory, cacheless, multiprocessor composed of 400 machines rated at 1 Teraflops. The network is a very low latency, high bandwidth network that attempts to keep 400 data streams active continuously from main memory to the individual processors.
- *Category 2:* A network of high-performance workstations with a hierarchical memory, including local memory or cache at every processor, This architecture follows the current trend of massively parallel

computers, and will have between 4,000 and 40,000 processors, each rated between 10 and 100 Gigaflops.

- *Category 3:* A multi-dimensional grid of hybrid chips that combine multiple processors and memory. This architecture is suitable for applications that can use fine-grain parallelism. It represents the evolution of architectures based on active memories. It will have approximately 100,000 to 1,000,000 processors, each rated at 400 Megaflops to 4 Gigaflops. Memory in this system is highly partitioned.

Some of the characteristics of the respective processor designs are summarized in Table 6.1. They are suited for different types of applications. The Category I machine is ideally suited for applications that create streams of accesses at easily predicted addresses. Typical of these applications are vector and matrix computations that access data with a uniform stride. This type of machine represents the evolutionary development of a CRAY 1 architecture. Because this architecture provides high connectivity and uniform latency, address references can range throughout shared memory, provided that streams of references from different machines are not conflicting.

Category II machines are multiprocessors that are useful for unstructured computations that exhibit a high degree of locality. Such machines might be useful for query systems and database applications where searches and record accesses tend to be clustered in time or to particular regions of the database. Address references in this architecture can be made anywhere in the hierarchy, but references to local memory are much less costly than references made to remote regions of memory. Consequently, performance depends strongly on how the architecture and software support together can successfully direct the majority of references to local data.

Category III machines take advantage of the high bandwidth of memory arrays internal to a memory chip, and provide bandwidth required to run a 400 Teraflops machine with substantially fewer parts than do either Category I or Category II machines. The performance potential can be achieved provided the applications make use of the local memory bandwidth, and have relatively little need to access data off-chip. For applications that can meet these constraints, Category III machines offer extremely low cost per Gigaflops.

Table 6.1
Characteristics of Design Points

Attribute	Category I	Category II	Category III
Type	Global Shared Memory	Distributed, Local	Active memory
Capacity	1 Byte/flops	1 Byte/flops	10^{-3} Bytes/flops
Bandwidth	1 Word/Sec/flops	1 Word/Sec/flops (cache) 0.1 to 0.5 Words/Sec/flops (off-chip) 10^{-2} Words/Sec/flops (global)	1 Word/Sec/flops (local) 10^{-3} Words/Sec (local)
Contention	Pure endpoint	Throughout hierarchy	Mainly chip-to-chip
Memory	400 Terabytes SRAM	400 Terabytes DRAM	800 Gigabytes DRAM
Chip density	2 GBytes/chip	8 GBytes/chip	8 GBytes/chip
Chip bandwidth	16 GBytes/sec/chip	160 Mbytes/sec/chip to 1.6 Gbytes/sec/chip (cache)	32 Tbytes/sec/chip (internal) 1.6 GBytes/sec/chip (external)
Memory chip count	200,000	50,000	100 (but will be located on CPU chips)
Processor performance	1 Teraflops/sec	10 Gigaflops to 100 Gigaflops	1 Gigaflops
Number of CPUs	400	4000 to 40,000	400,000
Chips/CPU	100	1 to 10	1/100 (No memory)
Processor chip count	40,000	4,000 to 40,000	4,000
Network chip count	1,000	5,000	0
Total chip count	250,000	60,000 to 100,000	4,000
Percentage memory	80	50 to 90	10 to 30 (of chip area)

Table 6.1 makes clear several important observations:

1. The major cost of Category I and II machines is for the memory. The reason that Category III machines have such low parts count is that they achieve the necessary bandwidth to sustain an aggregate rate of 400 Teraflops with a fraction of the number of memory parts by using the internal bandwidth of memory rather than the external bandwidth.

   Such machines can be used for applications that run effectively with a memory capacity much smaller than that postulated by the rule that says that memory capacity should be approximately one Gigabyte per Gigaflops per second of performance. The success of Category III machines will depend strongly on how widely this rule holds. If many applications need much less memory than prescribed by this rule, then the Category III machine will be an effective machine design. However, the range of applications that can make effective use of Category III machines has not been explored at this writing.

2. For both Category I and II machines, the cost of providing network bandwidth appears to be small compared to the cost of providing 400 Terabytes of memory. Consequently, the designs can afford to put various enhancements into interconnections to improve performance because the speed leverage they provide may be greater than proportional to their cost.

3. The table shows that Category I machines have a concurrency of 400, and produce $400 \cdot 10^{12}$ outputs per second. Therefore, it follows from the Concurrency Law that the latency must be no greater than 10^{-12} seconds (1 picosecond) per operation. If this latency is not achieved, each processor must have internal concurrency to offset the extra latency. Thus, if the output rate of an arithmetic unit is 1 output per nanosecond, each processor must have 1000 arithmetic units running at full speed in order for the system of 400 processors to output at a 400 Teraflops rate.

   By similar reasoning, if memory feeds processors at the rate of $400 \cdot 10^{12}$ operands per second, and the number of concurrent streams is 400, then the latency per stream can not be more than 10^{-12} seconds per memory stream. If the latency is N picoseconds per access, then $400N$ memory streams must run concurrently.

Table 6.2
Latency characteristics of design points

Attribute	Category I	Category II	Category III
Cache Memory Latency		10 to 100 ns	
Local Memory Latency		20 ns to 1 μs	1 μs
Global Memory Latency	1 ps	100 ns to 1 μs	1 ms

Table 6.2 gives the latency required for a single memory reference stream per processor. If actual latency exceeds the figure in the table by a factor N, then N accesses must be in progress concurrently.

6.3 Role of Device Technology

This section discusses device technology and its significance with respect to the possibility of building a Petaflops machine in about 20 years—assuming that device technology continues the same trend in the future that is has taken in the past.

Since memory costs are predominant in two of the three design studies, consider the Semiconductor Industry of America (SIA) data for future technology. Figure 6.4 shows projected chip density following a straight line on a semilog scale for the next several years. The SIA projections stop at the year 2007 when feature sizes are sufficiently small to cause tunneling effects, although newer data from SIA cited earlier suggests that technology advances will continue beyond 2007, although then it is not clear what direction technology will take. Nevertheless, if lithography and feature sizes continue to diminish for whatever new technology comes along, the projections out to the year 2014 produce densities high enough for the construction of a Petaflops machine at reasonable cost.

These projections account for a doubling in density in each linear dimension (quadrupling of density overall) every three years. A rough rule of thumb is a 10 times increase in density every five years, so that 20 years should produce a net of 10^4 increase in density and a corresponding decrease in parts count. The parts numbers tabulated in the previous section are quite manageable, and indicate that in 20 years the Petacomputer will cost about what a supercomputer costs today.

These findings are based on the previously noted crucial assumption that the technology road map can be extended beyond 2007, and there-

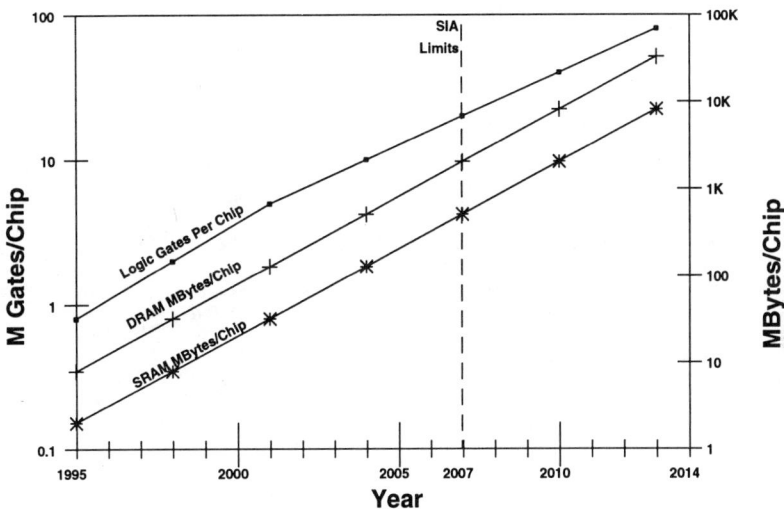

Figure 6.4
Projected circuit density for semiconductor technology

fore depend on a device technology that involves a tunneling phenomenon or some other physical phenomenon to produce a family of devices that do not yet exist.

Figure 6.5 shows parts counts as a function of memory density. These parts counts are valid for Category I and II designs if the memory capacity of a Petaflops computer follows the scaling law of one Gigabyte of main memory for each Gigaflops of performance for applications in the Petaflops region; otherwise, a design can make use of less main memory. Since memory costs are a major factor, a reduction in the required size of main memory would have a significant impact on the design. This impact is evident in the Category III design.

Figure 6.6 shows the total bandwidth available as a function of chip count. Note the dotted vertical line that shows the bandwidth available at the pins of memory chip in 1994. The figure also indicates low and high values for the internal bandwidth of a memory chip, which measures the number of bits activated during each memory cycle. In typical memory chips, from 1 to 8 bits are transmitted off-chip for each memory access. Memory itself is laid out in two dimensions, with rows and

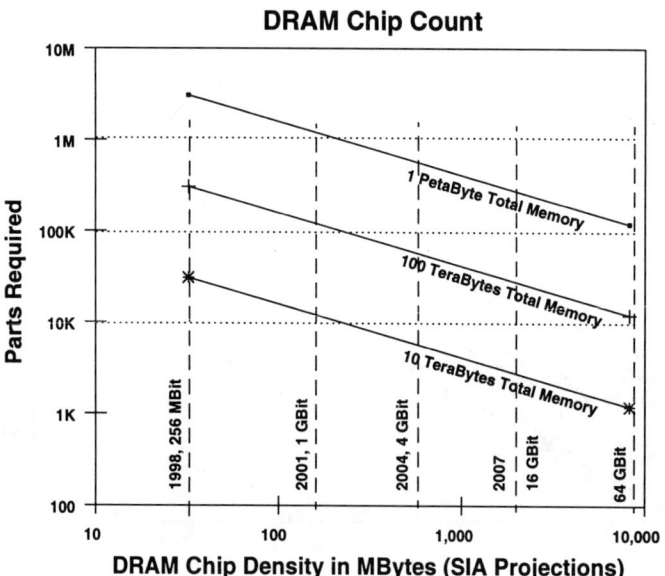

Figure 6.5
Parts count for SIA projected memory density

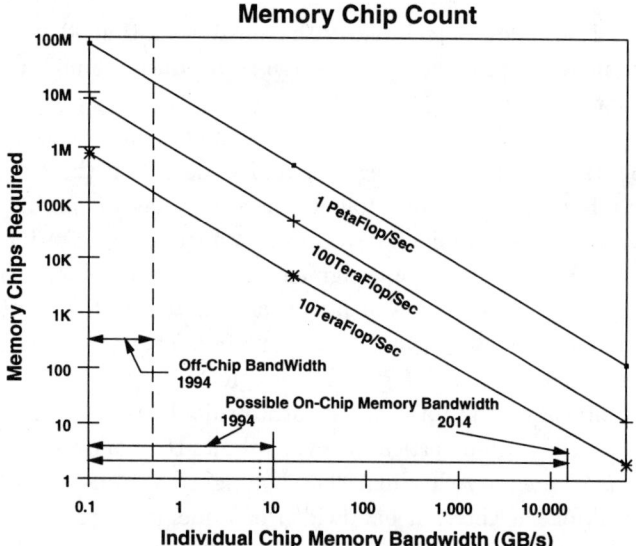

Figure 6.6
SIA Bandwidth projections for semiconductor technology

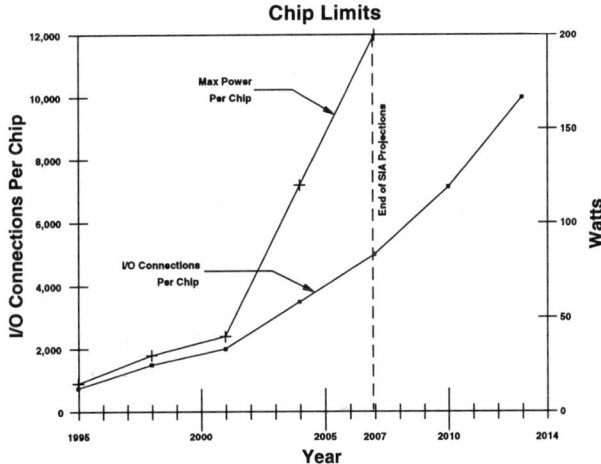

Figure 6.7
SIA power and I/O bandwidth per pin

columns of approximately equal size. An access selects one entire row of the chip, and reads this row into buffers. From the buffers, the access mechanism selects the 1 to 8 bits to be sent off-chip. Since rows and columns are of equal size, a typical N-bit chip is organized into an array that is $\sqrt{N} \times \sqrt{N}$, and thus $\sqrt{N}$ bits are accessed for each group of up to 8 bits sent off chip. In 1994, memory sizes have reached 16 Mbits per chip, so that 4096 bits are accessed for each set of up to 8 bits sent off chip. Because for some chips only a single bit is sent off chip per access, from 500 to 4000 times the internal bandwidth is discarded. Category III machines attempt to gain performance by using the internal bandwidth to drive processors colocated with the memory chips.

Cooling and external bandwidth per chip are both important factors in devices, and have a major impact on device counts for the Petaflops machine. Figures 6.7 and 6.8 show the SIA projections through 2007 and the panel's projections beyond that.

The SIA projections and the extrapolations through 2014 indicate that computer architecture as we know it today can support the design and construction of a Petaflops machine in 2014. Technology in the next 20 years will bring a substantial decrease in cost and risk in the design

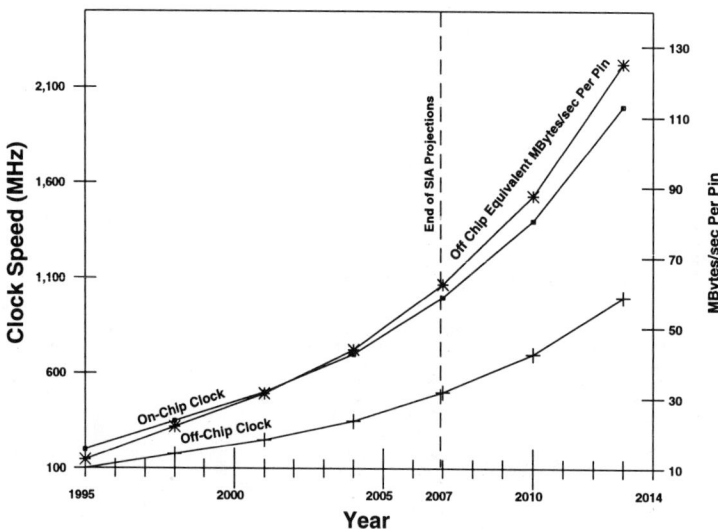

Figure 6.8
SIA projections for clock rates

and construction of such a machine. It is possible to build a Petaflops machine today, but with extraordinary cost—perhaps in the hundreds of billions of dollars—and at great risk of failure because of the enormous number of parts required. As projected costs drop (by a factor of 10 every five years), the cost of a Petacomputer drops to tens of millions in 20 years, well within the limits of supercomputers today. Also, the parts count in 2014 reduces to parts counts achieved today in large-scale machines.

6.4 Obstacles and Uncertainties

This exercise projected the SIA technology road map into realms where no device technology is known to operate. This suggests avenues of study of devices with feature sizes below 0.1 μm and raises issues regarding tunneling and other phenomena that become dominant in this regime.

Fundamental assumptions in the sizing of Category I and II designs are that memory requirements grow proportionally with performance, and that memory bandwidth grows proportionally also. These assumptions created a need for large memories for Category I and II machines, and the cost of the memory dominated the cost of the machine. This memory cost leaves very little room for the designer to lower cost through architectural advances. When these assumptions are abandoned, however, the Category III machine becomes a viable candidate, and it clearly has a cost advantage over the other types of machines.

It is essential to investigate memory requirements of large-scale applications to determine if memory capacity and bandwidth both scale linearly with performance. Markedly less expensive Category I and II designs may be possible if, for a large number of applications, the requirements scale less than linearly, resulting in smaller memories.

Market forces also will have a dramatic impact on the ability to build a Petaflops machine. The SIA technology curves are based on what is *likely* to be possible to build with the improvement of technology, but they do not predict what actually will be built. To keep costs per device at a minimum, the Petaflops machine should use the same memory and processor chips used in the mainstream to the extent possible. Because memory parts dominate Category I and II designs, the memory parts for these designs should be the same as those used in lower performance machines. Market forces, though, may slow the progress of commercial offerings so that they do not advance as rapidly as the SIA curves indicate might be possible. The effect of slower mainstream progress may either delay the viability of the Petaflops machine, or increase its cost, or both.

Memory bandwidth offers a particularly interesting challenge. The Category III design shows it is possible to tap existing bandwidth through an appropriate architectural design, but this technique is not unique. Memory manufacturers are starting to introduce memory schemes that raise the bandwidth per pin. Such schemes include synchronous memory devices and memory devices with built-in caches and synchronous block transfer modes.

Technology for the Petaflops machine should draw upon mainstream technology as much as possible. For special niches, however, it may be necessary to develop techniques that have little use beyond the Petaflops machine. As an example of such a niche, consider the Category

II and Category III designs, where the number of processors grows very large compared to today's highly parallel machines. Applications and systems software have a great challenge ahead to tap the power of high-speed machines by using 10,000-way parallelism effectively. It is not clear that today's programming paradigms will support efficient use of such machines. The vector and array codes may present some difficulty in partitioning them into 10,000 or more concurrent pieces. Writing multiprocessor programs with 10,000-way parallelism for less structured problems is an art that has rarely, if ever, been practiced. Consequently, the panel recommends that software technologists study parallelism techniques that will scale up to thousands and tens of thousands of processors.

The Petaflops machine appears to be destined to have a large diameter as defined earlier in this section. Hence, it has the potential for having larger latency and for suffering relatively more from latency than will machines with a smaller diameter (and lower average latency). For this reason, we need more effective techniques for latency hiding than we know today.

The very high parts count of the Petaflops machine may demand a special packaging and cooling technology that is not necessary for machines with substantially fewer parts.

Input/output requirements have not been addressed in this section because of a general belief that I/O requirements do not scale linearly with computational performance. For many large-scale algorithms, the number of operations grows much faster than linearly in the size of the input data. Consequently, the time it takes to calculate results must necessarily be much larger than the time it takes to load the initial data and write the results.

Nevertheless, peak I/O rates may be quite large. Also, some classes of problems have a computational requirement that scales linearly with the size of the problem. These classes clearly will place very high I/O demands on a Petaflops machine if they themselves scale large enough to demand Petaflops performance.

In reexamining the three categories of machines independently, the panel made the following observations:

- For the Category I machine, the main issue is memory. How big should it be? How can it be made very large, and still achieve low latency and high bandwidth?
- For the Category II machine, memory remains a major issue, but coupled with it is the requirement that the programs and data be partitioned to take advantage of local memory. The study and practice of automatic partitioning is only beginning.
- For the Category III machines, the main issue is how to write programs that can meet the very tight constraints placed on them by the architecture. Memory is constrained in total size. Extraordinarily high bandwidth is available for a selected set of data. If accesses need to go outside this set, the memory latency can increase by two or three orders of magnitude. This architecture poses a very interesting challenge to the algorithm developer.

6.5 Final Comments

For all three categories of machines, there is significant freedom in designing the processors. The results of design choices will have little impact on the final costs of the machines, but could have a very large impact on the performance. Given that it is possible to design a Petaflops machine, the implementation depends on successes in other areas. Device technology has to advance in the years after 2007. Programming technology has to develop paradigms and tools that scale to the development of programs for 10,000 processor machines. Applications programs have to based on models that lend themselves well to partitioning or streaming, and that can be cast in forms compatible with latency hiding and latency removal.

These challenges should result in feedback to the architecture community that helps guide the details of what can and should be put into future processors. The possible choices are virtually limitless. The relative costs of one method versus another may be very small. What is not known is which choices are good and which choices are not. To evaluate the choices, the architects need guidance from the device technologists regarding the characteristics of devices that will become available, and from the applications and systems programmers regarding what features make programs more efficient on machines in the Petaflops range.

Working together, the various teams should be able to achieve significant progress in the years to come.

6.6 Acknowledgments

The workshop panel is indebted to Peter Kogge for the figures used in this section, and to Peter Kogge, Tom Blank, and Burton Smith for substantial contributions to the written text.

Participants:

Harold S. Stone (chair)	IBM Research
Thomas Sterling (co-chair)	CESDIS, NASA GSFC
David Barkai	NASA Ames Research Center
Tom Blank	MasPar Computer Corp.
Seymour Cray	Cray Computer Corp.
Peter M. Kogge	IBM Federal Systems
A. Ray Miller	National Security Agency
Steve Nelson	Cray Research, Inc.
Greg Papadopoulos	Thinking Machines Corporation
John Pinkston	National Security Agency
Justin Rattner	Intel SSD
Burton Smith	Tera Computer Company

7 Software Technology Working Group: System Software and Tools

7.1 Introduction

Software technology is the system component that bridges the gap between applications and computing hardware. As such, it includes tools for application development as well as software components that regulate system operation and the allocation of system resources. The former category includes compilers, debuggers, and program performance analyzers; the latter category includes the various operating-system functions such as scheduling, file systems, input/output systems, communication, security, and protection from errant user programs. On top of the actual hardware system, these components combine to build a "virtual system" that ideally is effective and pleasant for programmers and end-users to use, and also makes efficient use of the underlying hardware resources.

In the case of high-performance and especially massively parallel computing, the need for such a "virtual system" is all the more acute because the bare hardware for such machines is increasingly complex and challenging to use effectively. However, software technology alone, as a discipline, is limited in the effective transformation it can achieve from raw iron to virtual system. It can only deliver efficient hardware utilization when methods for achieving that utilization are known and can be reduced to an algorithmic form. Even when such methods are known, software technology can apply them to a given application program only when the program is presented in a form that enables the software technology to extract the information needed to apply the methods correctly.

This chapter considers the role of software technology for Petaflops-scale computation. Issues addressed include the implications of highly parallel hardware structures, the requirement for establishing a virtual system that is both easy to program and yields sufficient performance, critical elements of software technology for Petaflops systems, and advanced computing environments from which new ways of using highly parallel systems may emerge. A key finding is that system development must include software technology at the outset and that hardware design must reflect the needs of system software, not just the other way around.

7.2 The Challenge of Software Technology

The peak performance of the raw system hardware is transformed to usable or sustainable performance of the virtual system that is presented to the programmer by the intervening system software. One of the main obstacles facing high-performance computing (HPC) is that the trade-off between usability and delivered performance is so steep. The challenge of software technology is to lessen the trade-off gradient and achieve good performance from relatively easy-to-program systems and near-peak performance through moderately greater programming effort. This challenge is already formidable in the domain of Teraflops computing and, should current trends continue, looks nearly insurmountable at the Petaflops level for all but an extremely specialized range of applications. Building Petaflops systems that can be used successfully for a wide range of applications will require innovative models, methods, and tools that go beyond conventional practice.

A difficulty in the area of the software technology is defining quantitative, meaningful, and measurable metrics of the value delivered to users. Such metrics need to capture two important determinants of value: cost and benefit.

- Cost has two major dimensions:
  - Capital investment can be measured fairly easily, although we should bear in mind that the capital invested in a supercomputer often can be quite different from the "list price" of a benchmark system, because of factors such as discounts, installation costs, add-on hardware, and the costs of connecting users to the system.
  - Human investment includes not only "direct" costs such as the effort required to develop an application program, but also indirect costs such as support and improvement of the program after it is initially written (which can exceed the original development cost), the time taken by end users to learn how to use the application effectively for their purposes, and the investment in education and training for both programmers and end users.

- Benefit encompasses several rather intangible factors that are difficult to quantify. These include:
  - The value of solving an application problem at a given quality level (as compared with the value of a different-quality solution that could be achieved at a different cost).
  - The value of obtaining the solution to an application problem within a given time frame.

When all these dimensions of value are considered, the reasons for many frequently seen trade-offs become more evident. For example, there is almost always a trade-off between reducing computing time (capital investment) and reducing programming time (human investment). The human investment is often the more significant, especially for a program that may only be run a few times before being changed. As a consequence, some application developers persist in using regular grids and straightforward algorithms even at the cost of much longer execution times: they use more computer time but need much less program development time. Similarly, hardware or software providing a global address space can be used, relaxing the burden on programmers to perform data layout but at the expense of increased execution time or system cost. If the metrics do not reflect these factors then the justification for such decisions will go unobserved.

There has been a tendency in the development of the HPC field—and particularly where massive parallelism is concerned—to focus attention on the development of raw hardware capabilities and relegate to software technology the job of converting these raw capabilities into delivered value for users. Software technology is required to bridge an ever-widening gap between hardware-supplied capabilities and user needs as the scale of hardware parallelism expands. The added complexity that appears when hardware offers parallelism at many levels and the disparity of resource access times across distributed systems only aggravate the difficulty. Success in bridging this gap requires that software technologists work together with hardware architects and application specialists in defining the interfaces between their respective domains.

7.3 Technology Trends and Strategic Opportunities

There is no technology road map for software innovation. However, some disturbing trends are clear. First, the software for the current generation of 100 Gigaflops machines is not adequate to be scaled to a Teraflops and it will certainly fail on a Petaflops system. With the possible exception of the proposed High Performance Fortran (HPF), supercomputing system software and environments are seriously underfunded and underdeveloped. More specifically, multi-user operating systems, truly scalable I/O, and portable programming and debugging tools are, with a few notable exceptions, missing from scalable parallel systems being built today.

An important factor contributing to this condition is the conventional vision of the way in which supercomputers including a Petaflops machine would be used. Traditionally we have built supercomputers that had little software because there was a large market in the national laboratories for machines with very high performance and very specialized use. These machines were more like large laboratory instruments than general-purpose computers. This trend has accelerated as large-scale parallel systems have proved to be the only way to achieve the speed levels envisioned for future applications. As a result, software has to be especially targeted for these systems and will be used by a relatively small community.

A second factor is that parallel machines suffer from greater performance instability than sequential systems. Consequently, if a machine is not designed with the problems of software in mind, only a few highly tuned programs will achieve high efficiency. One reason for this is the inability of many systems to assist software in hiding memory latency or exploiting the nested and dynamic forms of parallelism that some applications require. In addition, memory-system considerations will require a Petaflops machine to have at least a million operations active in parallel at all times to achieve the system's full speed and prevent memory latencies due to distance, access times, and bank contention from starving processing resources. Realistic memory-design assumptions will very likely push this parallelism requirement one or more orders of magnitude higher. System software and programming methods will be required to take on the added burden of exposing enormous program parallelism and coordinating activities on a grand scale. Thus, a Petaflops system, unless properly designed, will be even more difficult to program than current systems.

If current trends are permitted to extend into the future, significant contributions by independent software vendors (ISVs) will be precluded. These trends result in systems for which it will be difficult to develop efficient new programs, port existing programs, or find a significant user community. ISVs cannot afford to port their products to large-scale parallel systems if a heroic effort is required for each new machine. Software technology for MPP's must evolve new ways to design software that is portable across a wide variety of computer architectures. Only then can the small but important MPP sector of the computer hardware market leverage the massive investment that is being applied to commercial software for the business and commodity computer market.

Over the next 20 years, the Grand Challenge applications of today will evolve to resemble multidisciplinary scientific virtual laboratories demanding a complex mix of simulation, human interaction, and multimedia scaled far beyond what is possible today. These will be joined by a second class of applications that can be characterized as the compute-intensive component of the National Information Infrastructure (NII). These NII applications will use Petaflops systems as vast million-user information and analysis resources. These applications will not be easy to design with a pure data-parallel model. However, techniques that integrate the efficiency of data parallelism with the flexibility of distributed object systems are starting to emerge and they relate directly to the software directions being taken for the NII at large.

Finally, the economic foundations for sustainable development of HPC technology over the long term will be based on the power of the marketplace to focus resources on commercially valuable and viable technology. To the extent that the development of software technology for HPC can ride this wave, progress can be greatly accelerated. To the extent that it cannot, HPC software technology evolution will progress more slowly than mainstream software technology. Historically, HPC software efforts have not been cross-subsidized through the leveraging of investments in other sectors of the computer market and consequently they have been underfunded. The resulting parallel software supplied by HPC vendors and others lacks the robustness and polish found in software aimed at the commercial world. Only an expanded market will give vendors the resources to improve matters. To succeed at this, the hardware and software of such systems (1) must target applications that ultimately have the potential to be commercially self-sustaining and (2) must implement a common set of programming models and methods to support portability of applications between different vendors' systems. This latter point is a precondition to attracting serious interest from independent software vendors.

7.4 BLISS versus the Metasystem: Two Visions of Petaflops Computing

The choices we face in mapping out the development of Petaflops computing technology can be brought into focus by considering two development paths, which are the two ends of a spectrum of opportunities. The first path continues the high-performance-computer-as-big-laboratory-instrument approach mentioned above. We may refer to the software technology required for this approach as BLISS (Big Lab Instrument Software System). BLISS is specifically oriented toward scientific computing on "big iron" machines. The second path leads to the development of a seamless "metasystem," composed of multiple high-performance (but sub-Petaflops) machines, designed for use by a wide community. This path leverages the commercial software market by providing the software infrastructure needed to facilitate (entice) the entry of ISVs into the parallel processing market. Below, we expand on these two diametrically opposed visions, examine their respective impact on technology, and discuss the risks and rewards associated with each.

BLISS represents the status quo in which the abstract machine presented to the programmer closely matches the underlying physical machine. The system will be response-time oriented and targeted to data-parallel scientific applications. It will be a single-user, batch-style environment, with resource management being performed primarily by hand. With the exception of data-parallel applications, writing software on BLISS will be at least as difficult as it is today on comparable systems. Current tools, or reasonable extensions to these tools (e.g., HPF), will provide the software infrastructure for data-parallel programming. As noted above, the range of applications for which these tools are effective is likely to become narrower and narrower as peak system performance increases, unless software and hardware architects collaborate to reverse this trend.

The construction of a seamless metasystem is a departure from current mainstream trends in high-performance computing. With the exception of regular, data-parallel problems, it is already too difficult to write applications for parallel machines; this problem will severely handicap attempts to broaden the marketplace. Much of the problem stems from the fact that the programmer of massively parallel systems today is exposed fully to the underlying machine and must constantly manage the details of where, when, and how computations are performed. The solution is to hide these details, allowing the programmer to concentrate on the application, not on low-level implementation details. This is accomplished by providing various forms of transparency—access, location, and temporal transparency, to name a few. We envision a software system with the following properties:

- It is easy to use. Resource management and scheduling are transparent and automatic.

- It is multilayered. At higher levels of abstraction, the system would manage most details for the programmer (possibly at some cost in computing time), but lower levels of abstraction permitting a greater degree of manual control are also available.

- It possesses an interactive, multimedia front end.

- It supports mixed-language applications.

- It stresses software reuse by encouraging the use of object-based abstractions that mask implementation details. The abstractions can be re-used and extended by programmers without requiring them to become intimate with the implementation.

- It supports multiple simultaneous users and is accessible to a wide community.

- It stresses both throughput and response time. Since the metasystem has a large user community, it must function efficiently as a throughput engine, concurrently processing unrelated user jobs. However, when response time is paramount, it must be possible to recruit a "task force" consisting of an appropriate number of processors to execute a single application with the desired degree of parallelism.

Continued development of current tools and approaches, but little else, is required to build BLISS. The software technology for a seamless metasystem, however, will depart radically from current HPC software in many ways. Work is needed in the areas of programming models, parallel languages, language interaction, compilers and run-time support, resource management, user interfaces and tools, and I/O and database management. A major effort is needed in operating systems—the nature and scale of the challenges faced by the operating system for a metasystem will make it quite different from operating systems as we have known them for the last 20 years.

BLISS is a well-understood design philosophy, with well-understood pitfalls, and with comparatively small up-front software development costs. Software costs with BLISS are not low, though. Instead, they are distributed to the users, recurring, and hidden: software development for all but data-parallel applications will continue to be extremely painful.

The risks associated with metasystem development are much greater. There is a significant up-front software investment that is not guaranteed to bear fruit. Also, for those applications that would run well under BLISS, execution on the metasystem is likely to entail a performance penalty, further increasing the gap between peak (guaranteed never to exceed) performance, and realized performance for those applications. On the plus side, the metasystem will be accessible and useful to a larger class of users and applications, not just traditional "number crunching," and it has more potential to leverage the commercial software market by facilitating a transition to parallel computing by commercial software vendors. Further, the metasystem presents an opportunity to realize a Petaflops system sooner by interconnecting many sub-Petaflops systems. In the final analysis, for parallel computers to become commercially viable requires that they be made easier to use, and thus become mainstream. Without moving away from the laboratory-instrument model, that will not happen.

Since both BLISS and the metasystem are extremes on a spectrum, the most likely scenarios fall somewhere between them. However, we believe that the HPC usage models that are likely to be self-sustaining and viable over the long term fall closer to the metasystem end of the spectrum. Moreover, the explosive proliferation of high-performance wide-area networking technology virtually guarantees that any Petaflops machine will be born into a computational world that is already organized into a metasystem of some sort. For a Petaflops system to operate effectively in this world, its design will have to take into account many of the considerations outlined above. Therefore, although we do not altogether abandon the BLISS model in the discussions that follow, we will be particularly mindful of the technology directions required for the metasystem approach.

7.5 Discussion of Software Technology Areas

Software technology is a broad, diverse area. This section discusses the major subcategories of this technology area and outlines the current status, major trends, opportunities, and barriers to progress in each. There are substantial software technology problems that have not been solved satisfactorily even on the scale of Teraflops, let alone Petaflops. In general, we will focus on trends and problems that need attention, without regard to where in the Teraflops-Petaflops range the problems become severe.

Some Petaflops applications can be expected to be the lineal descendants of today's HPC scientific computations, while others will be new to the HPC sphere. Many of these latter applications will emphasize computing and information retrieval on massive data sets. Even among the scientific computations, we expect to see a shift toward a greater emphasis on computations whose structure evolves dynamically at run time (such as modern N-body simulation algorithms) and/or which have nested levels of parallelism, which are not handled well by implementation strategies based on statically computed mapping and resource-allocation decisions. Data-intensive applications are likely to exhibit these characteristics to an even greater extent, leading to new demands on software technology. These observations form our point of departure for the following discussion.

Programming Languages and Models

Programming languages and models are the notations and underlying concepts used for writing programs. Although there is not a sharp dividing line, we can distinguish two kinds of programming methods: building software "from scratch" is one, and assembling software by "wiring together" pre-existing modules, with comparatively little customization, is the other. This section focuses on technology supporting the former method; technology for the latter is discussed in the next section under "Programming Technology."

Generally, programmers have been able to use Fortran and message passing to produce multiprocessor implementations of scientific and engineering codes that do not require particularly high-performance I/O. Some classes of codes have also proved to be amenable to the commercial predecessors of HPF—CM Fortran and MasPar Fortran. These efforts have been the most successful in the case of dense matrix codes, but programming costs are still high and portability is low. We are also making progress in developing tools for some limited domains of sparse matrix computations, but this is still a struggle. Except for massively parallel, coarse-grain, regular programs, execution speeds are often slower than comparable programs running on vector supercomputers and developed at less cost.

Parallelizing compilers have not achieved the initially expected success. There are still ongoing efforts to parallelize code and also automatically distribute data for distributed memory machines. Even though these efforts may achieve good performance for small kernels, it is not clear (at least up to now) how successful they can be for full programs, which tend to be large and have complicated logic.

For more detailed discussion, it is best to subdivide the broad area of programming languages and models into several (overlapping) categories as follows:

- Data-parallel programming models and languages. Traditionally this model has meant lock-step parallel processing of dense vector and array data, without task parallelism or nested parallelism. Ideas such as segmented scans have extended the domain of this model somewhat, and perhaps a more general way to characterize it today is "parallelism with a low diversity of instruction mix." This model is exemplified by C*, Fortran D, Vienna Fortran, HPF and pC++, as well as lower-level programming tools for SIMD machines, such as MasPar's MPL. Vector- and matrix-oriented, but not overtly parallel, programming languages like Fortran 90 and APL also may be considered to fall within this category. However, of the above languages, only HPF is being implemented commercially as a portable programming language for parallel machines. Since HPF implementations are only starting to appear, its potential will not be known for some time.

- Although the majority of successes in massively parallel processing have come from the use of the data-parallel model, there is concern that it cannot handle highly dynamic or irregular computations gracefully, and therefore the range of applications that it can handle may be limited. Nevertheless, it probably will be possible to port effectively a significant subset of scientific and engineering codes using data-parallel language extensions such as HPF (and related extensions for irregular problems).

- Shared-memory programming models and languages. These are traditionally models in which all data is equally accessible to all computations, without regard to where in the machine the data may have been placed or where a computation may be performed. Examples include thread packages such as Presto, and the technologies that have been used for programming quasi-shared-memory machines such as the Stanford DASH, MIT Alewife, and Kendall Square Research KSR-1 machines.

- Generally, the shared-memory model is viewed as the easiest model for programmers to use, but it is often felt to be inappropriate for massively parallel computing because it hides communication operations. However, research into software-based distributed shared memory techniques continues, with some promising results at moderate scales of parallelism. Also, hardware architectures such as the DASH, Alewife, KSR-1, and Tera computers suggest other ways of scaling up the shared-memory model. It should be noted that data-parallel languages like HPF (or Fortran 90) and functional languages like Sisal may also be seen as instances of the shared-memory computing model in that they hide communication operations (or at least make them less explicit).

- Distributed-memory ("message passing") programming models and languages. In contrast to shared-memory models, distributed-memory models make the location of data and computations explicit, and require explicit, programmed communication actions to bring them together as needed. Examples include message-passing systems like PVM, Linda, P4, and Express. Unfortunately, developing large-scale parallel programs using these packages is very difficult and time-consuming. Currently, the MPI committee is trying to standardize a message-passing library, but although this may become a more widespread standard, it has essentially the same characteristics as the packages mentioned above. Linda offers higher-level communication and synchronization primitives but still requires the programmer to manage the mapping of data and computations to processors. Other languages that are available include Fortran-M (Argonne) and Merlin (ICASE).

- Functional programming models and languages. These models are based on programming without side effects. The premise is that eliminating side effects eliminates one of the major sources of difficulty in parallel programming (read-write and write-write timing races). The majority of functional languages guarantee deterministic execution, and in fact make it impossible to write nondeterministic programs. Sisal is one example of such a language. However, some "functional" languages include constructs such as non-deterministic stream merges that allow nondeterministic programs to be written. Although still viewed as experimental by much of the community, Sisal has proven to be able to support both optimization and expressivity. Higher-order functional languages add even more expressive power, but good performance in production situations is not yet demonstrated.

- Object-oriented programming models and languages. These are models based on the object-oriented abstraction capabilities of languages like Smalltalk and C++. Instead of simplifying parallel programming the way functional languages do (by eliminating side effects), object-oriented parallel programming models use the information-hiding character of the object abstraction as a simplifying principle: the limits on interaction between an object's users and its implementation reduce the number of interactions that a parallel programmer needs to worry about.

- Since some object-oriented programming models are explained in terms of sending "messages" to objects, one might think of object-oriented programming as a natural match for distributed-memory programming; however, a "message" sent to an object is fundamentally an abstraction—or logical communication—operation, whose purpose is quite different from the physical communication performed by messages in a distributed-memory computing model. In fact, object-oriented ideas can be used with any of the models mentioned above.

- Numerous interesting research and advanced development projects have been launched to extend C++ with some support for parallelism. These include COOL (Stanford), Mentat (Virginia), and Tera C++. However, none of these languages have been widely used yet.

In any scenario for Petaflops computing architectures, communications management emerges as a key issue. Some programming models, such as Fortran D and HPF, allow and/or require programmers to specify the location of data and/or computations. Other models automate these decisions. In the long run, with massively parallel machines and dynamic applications, programmer-controlled locality management may prove to be unworkable; on the other hand, automating this task with acceptable results across a broad range of applications still poses many research challenges. In any case, software technology will have to help with

- Locality management: minimizing communication by suitably allocating, replicating, and scheduling data and computations.

- Latency management: techniques such as prefetching and multithreading (fast context switching) to maintain computational speed even in the face of long communication or memory latencies.

Hardware support has often proven to be valuable here: examples include the use of cache memory and virtual memory for locality management in conventional computers. Latency management has a shorter history but is likely to become increasingly important as we move toward Petaflops. We need to understand better how hardware and software can help each other solve this problem.

Programming Technology

This category comprises programming aids that are not programming languages or models per se.

- Modularity and code reuse aids. Object-oriented programming models help separate module specifications from their implementations and thus promote modularity; however, even object-oriented programming does not guarantee code reuse. More progress needs to be made in the development of tools and programming styles that help programmers to build modules that are likely to be reusable and to find existing reusable modules that will serve their needs.

- Toolkits. For mundane applications, programming in the classical sense is becoming rarer as more and more "programming" tasks are done using tools such as spreadsheets, database query languages, user-interface builders, and the like. Although such tools are not as general-purpose as conventional programming languages, they are very useful within their particular domains of applicability, and since they allow the user to deal with higher-level concepts and modules, they offer opportunities to incorporate parallel processing transparently. In 1994, such toolkits play only a negligibly small role in HPC software development, but we think a quiet revolution is possible and likely over the next 20 years, resulting in a much higher level of toolkit-driven application development for Petaflops machines. This revolution should be encouraged, as it is one of the more promising fresh ideas on the horizon for leap-frogging the problems of moving conventional programming technology onto highly parallel systems such as Petaflops computers.

- Performance analysis and optimization. Understanding and tuning the performance of even moderately parallel programs is already a major challenge. We will need better tools in this area to make effective use of Petaflops systems. Today, research systems such as Pablo, ParaGraph, and IPS-2 can capture and present detailed performance data from explicitly parallel, distributed-memory codes and high-level data from shared-memory codes. We lack the ability to analyze and present data for data-parallel languages. Likewise, we cannot easily accommodate thousands of processors without sacrificing either measurement detail or inducing large perturbations in observed behavior. We also lack the ability to tune complex, heterogeneous parallel codes effectively. Finally, we need to do a better job of understanding the real needs of tool users, and bridging the cultural gap between them and tool developers, so that the tools that are developed will actually be valuable to the tool users.

Input/Output

This is frequently mentioned as an important area where parallel systems need to improve, but actually taking action to improve I/O is often postponed. We can consider this problem in a couple of pieces:

- Data storage. It is sobering to consider the data-set and working-storage (i.e., RAM) size for Petaflops computations. If a Petaflops machine needs on the order of a Petabyte of working storage, then if we want to dump this storage to disk (or its equivalent) in a time on the order of 15 minutes or less, we will need an aggregate bandwidth to disk on the order of Terabytes per second! While providing this level of capability is a hardware issue, there is also the question of designing the interface presented to the compiler/programmer. Current systems make it difficult to tell the file system in advance what data is needed and where, even when the data distribution and access patterns are known. Further, type-specific access, caching, and prefetching mechanisms cannot be specified, limiting the programmer to the minimal interface provided by the operating system. To solve these problems, we first need to learn much more about the types of input/output that application developers need, versus the limits of what they exploit now due to hardware and system-software limitations.

- User interaction and visualization. The raw data resulting from a Petaflops computation will be too massive for a human being to assimilate directly. For example, if each pixel on a display screen represented the result from 100 floating-point operations, then a Petaflops machine could compute 10^7 1000 × 1000 display screens each second! As computer performance increases and human performance does not, there will be an increasing need for interactive data reduction, visualization, and "computation steering" tools to bridge the gap.

Suitable hardware infrastructure will be needed to support these input/output requirements, but software technology will have to manage it and make it easy to use.

Resource Management and Scheduling

The vast array of computational, storage, and input/output resources likely to be found on a Petaflops machine will heavily stress traditional operating-system functions such as task scheduling and resource allocation. Additionally, if a Petaflops machine is to be shared by multiple users (as in the "seamless metasystem" scenario), operating systems will need to provide the necessary protection between users without adding significant overhead to basic operations such as communication, synchronization, and task creation. The right hardware architecture can make these tasks easier, but the software still has to be structured to take advantage of the hardware.

Today's multiprocessor operating systems are primitive with respect to the needs of their users and (often) even with respect to the state of the art in uniprocessor operating systems. The following are some characteristics often seen in commercial multiprocessor operating systems:

- Support for only one user at a time.

- Manual resource allocation (e.g., static allocation of specific processors or memory areas to specific users).

- Poor or nonexistent locality management (e.g., shared-memory multiprocessor operating systems that freely move processes from one processor to another).

- No mechanism for feedback from overall system conditions to local resource-allocation decisions (e.g., suggesting that a program organize its work to use three processors because that is how many are currently free).

A great deal of work needs to be done in solving these and other similar problems if a Petaflops machine is to deliver anything even remotely close to the level of service that would be expected of a general-purpose "computing utility."

The Training and Experience Base of Scientific Program Developers

The scientific-programming community traditionally has used Fortran and now is moving toward greater use of C and C++. However, this community has in the past been extremely reluctant to adopt new programming paradigms. The previous sections illustrate many ways in which new paradigms have the potential to be more effective than traditional paradigms in exploiting Petaflops-class systems. We need to consider how to prepare the community to accept new paradigms when they prove to be effective.

7.6 Recommendations

Software technology is crucial to the success of Petaflops computing and requires substantial advances beyond conventional methods in two broad areas: technical and infrastructure. Technical advances are required in software technology to achieve sustained Petaflops performance for real-world application programs and to achieve a substantial reduction in the human effort required to yield the desired performance. These two areas, machine and human-resource effectiveness, are strongly connected and mutually supportive. Infrastructure changes are required to ensure sufficient and sustained funding of software development essential to the viability of Petaflops computing systems. Finally, it should be noted that two recent workshops [Messina:93d], [Smith:93a] have addressed the problems of software technology in the context of the Federal HPCC program. The recommendations of those reports apply directly to the Petaflops effort, with their urgency increased by a significant factor.

Machine-Effectiveness Recommendations

History has shown that as the degree of parallelism required to achieve a given level of hardware performance increases, the ability of users to use that parallelism effectively has decreased. A Petaflops computer would require, under the most conservative estimates, a parallelism factor of at least 1,000,000. This degree of parallelism is unprecedented from a software-technology point of view. To utilize such a system effectively, it is crucial for the users to have software-technology aids. The recommendations in this section address these concerns.

Significant work is needed in all areas related to handling the large data sets that will be required by Petaflops systems. Users must be able to express efficient I/O operations at a high level and have those operations mapped onto parallel hardware which supports parallel I/O. Tools must be developed to visualize these data sets in an interactive manner. The scale of data sets to be processed also will require significant advances in checkpoint and restart capabilities, as it is infeasible to checkpoint such large images by copying them in their entirety. The performance data on a user's program is, in itself, a tremendously large data set. Tools and hardware support must be developed to handle this data efficiently and effectively as well.

Another area for significant research and development is that of compilers and automatic program mapping. While data-parallel compilers have made advances in recent years, many of the applications discussed in this book are not well suited to that model because of their unstructured (or at least non-array-based) nature. Users must be better able to express their applications to the software support system so that the system (compilers, mappers, runtime support systems, etc.) can better match the resources available to the requirements of the users.

Some applications of Petaflops computing may require access by as many as a million simultaneous users of such a system. If this is to be achieved, a major push in operating system research would be required because such capability is unlikely to be derived through other research programs.

Human-Effectiveness Recommendations

To address the inadequate state of software productivity, there is a need to develop language systems able to integrate software components that use different paradigms and language dialects. No existing single parallelism model adequately covers the spectrum required by applications today. Future applications will require even greater diversity. We need to invest in efforts that recognize and merge the strengths of existing models. These models include object-oriented, functional, and HPF-style imperative programming. It is not sufficient to fund these efforts independently. Efforts must be undertaken to merge the styles intelligently and perform objective comparisons to determine their appropriate use.

Such comparisons must include comparisons of programming costs: we cannot afford parallel programming costs that are 4–5 times greater than sequential programming costs (and we can afford them even less if they are repeated for each new machine). A question that should be asked about every programming model or tool is, "Does it make developing a parallel program as easy as developing a sequential program?"

Because it is uncertain what form the final Petaflops platform will take (and in fact it may be heterogeneous itself), implementation of software technology across diverse platforms must be emphasized. Software systems must provide smooth migration from simple workstations to the most complex parallel systems. Software systems must be tuned to deal with all of these targets. Priority for investment should go to software systems that demonstrate minimal changes to source code when moving across diverse platforms, without serious losses in performance.

When evaluating software-technology projects targeted at Petaflops computing, emphasis should be placed on those projects providing interoperability amongst software tools. Most current software-tool efforts focus on providing help to specific applications. While valuable, these projects do not provide incentives or funding to make tools interoperable that were initially created for different projects. The same can be said for most tools developed in isolation from any application project. Software-technology projects aimed at Petaflops computing should stress the definition and use of flexible interface standards and/or extensible toolkits between layers of software (e.g., between compilers and debuggers, performance analysis tools and run-time systems, etc.). One way of achieving progress here would be to fund software efforts jointly with the explicit goal of interoperability between them.

To increase human effectiveness further, application-development toolkits must be designed and put into use by application writers. For Petaflops computing, we expect few applications to be built from scratch. To solve progressively more complex problems, application developers need an improved capability to define interfaces to their products so that other developers can reliably and efficiently use these products without detailed knowledge of their internal operation. For software-tool efforts that are closely aligned with particular applications, one required product should be the provision of a well-defined and readily available interface for public access.

Infrastructure Recommendations

Enhancements to the infrastructure contributing to software technology development are essential for realizing the goals of system performance and programmer effectiveness. Too often, software technology has not been treated as an essential enabler for highly parallel computing, on a par with hardware technology and application development. We must admit that there is a software problem and work to resolve it by addressing the following needs:

1. better interactions with both hardware and application developers,
2. improved paths for developing successful research software into robust tools for production use, and

3. broader education and training on parallel paradigms and tools.

The forum for interchange among application developers and system software designers must be expanded. Software designers need a better understanding of the future algorithm types and problem sizes that application developers have in mind. Application developers need a better understanding of when and how using optimizers can save them effort and when it will cost them performance. There is a particular need to fund "races" to see which combinations of application algorithms, software support, and computer systems can solve problems. The metrics for success must include the time to develop the code, the execution time of the program, and the amount of resources needed to get to a solution.

Moreover, just as software technologists need to listen carefully to application experts and focus on software technologies that can satisfy real application needs, application experts too need to listen carefully to software technologists and consider thoughtfully how they can benefit from the opportunities that software technologists see. To put it bluntly, it is commonplace today for the application side to constrain the solution (e.g., "It must be Fortran") as well as specifying the problem. Such a relationship obstructs the development and evaluation of the radical new software ideas that will be needed to reach Petaflops. We need better mechanisms for "far-out" or unfashionable software technology ideas to be developed fully enough that they can be evaluated fairly against real application needs.

Similarly, the forum for interchange among architecture designers and system-software designers must be expanded as well. Here the goal is to carefully study the trade-offs between the cost of putting features in hardware and software, where the appropriate cost measures also need to be defined. Areas where this approach is needed include: providing performance information (with programmable on-the-fly data reduction), effective hardware support for parallel I/O, handling of data layout and quick remote access (software technologists favor a single address space), and methods for reducing and/or hiding latency.

There is a critical need to promote the evolution of successful research prototypes into robust, "user-ready" systems. This recommendation follows closely a recommendation from both previous software technology workshops. Funding agencies must recognize the need to take successful research projects to the next level of robustness for production use by code developers. These transitions require substantially greater funding than the corresponding research funding (per project). Agencies can leverage some of these costs by encouraging the involvement of independent software vendors (through SBIRs and other similar vehicles) and requiring that research software be distributed (and used!) through software-exchange facilities. The long-range goal would be to transfer research software into profit-making products supported solely by companies.

Another approach that needs to be encouraged in this area is that of software "trickle-up." The current market for workstation and PC-based software is huge. While there is little applicability of software such as word processors and calendar managers to Petaflops computing, it may be possible to leverage this market in other ways. Particular areas of emphasis should be support for porting scientific applications, leveraging and influencing the emerging multiprocessor workstation compiler tools, and networked operating-system functions.

Finally, and perhaps most importantly, support is needed for expanded education and training on parallel paradigms and tools. Parallel computing is an enabling technology for an expanding set of application areas. The training of potential users must be broadened to include diverse models of parallelism and techniques for layerable and reliable system implementations. While Fortran (and its variations) is supported as one model, it should be included only as a part of a more comprehensive view of programming techniques.

7.7 Software Technology Conclusions

Policy makers, funding agencies, and technology forecasters have an understandable interest in quantifiable metrics, fundamental limits, levels of investment, rates of progress, and milestones; hence, it is natural for the qualitative and unpredictable nature of progress in software technology to cause frustration. The reasons why software technology is like this have been discussed above, along with the reasons why it is nonetheless a vital area in which progress is urgently needed.

In fact, there has been great progress in software technology over the last 40 years, but it has been episodic and (as always) difficult to quantify, which gives it quite a different character from the seemingly inexorable march of hardware technology. There is every reason to believe that continued software technology progress of the same kind is possible in the future, and that under the right conditions it can deliver urgently needed benefits in the realm of HPC up to and including Petaflops systems. This book has outlined the major areas of software technology in which progress is needed and possible. A key requirement for a good rate of progress is setting the proper context for software technology development, including (1) leveraging the commercial marketplace and (2) fostering strong working partnerships of software technologists with hardware architects and application specialists.

However, the software-technology challenges of supporting Petaflops computing rates over a broad spectrum of applications are indeed formidable, and meeting them will require innovative ideas, not just extensions of existing trends. Although committees can extrapolate trends with some success, the "break the mold" ideas that will allow us to reach the Petaflops goal will come from highly motivated and prepared individuals, not from committees. Investments such as those described in the preceding sections certainly will be important, but the most important investment that can be made is in attracting the right talents to focus their energies on HPC software technology and ensuring that they then have the resources needed to make effective contributions.

7.8 Acknowledgments

Participants:

Bill Carlson (Co-Chair)	Supercomputing Research Center
John Dorband	NASA Goddard
John Feo	Lawrence Livermore National Laboratory
Dennis Gannon	Indiana University
Andrew Grimshaw	University of Virginia
Bert Halstead (Chair)	Digital Equipment Corp.
Michael Heath	University of Illinois/NCSA

Monica Lam	Stanford University
Jim McGraw	Lawrence Livermore National Laboratory
Piyush Mehrotra	ICASE
Cherri Pancake	Oregon State University
Jim Pool	Caltech
Dan Reed	University of Illinois
Joel Saltz	University of Maryland

8 Major Findings

This first comprehensive review of the emerging field of Petaflops computing systems produced a number of important findings that broadly define the challenge, opportunities, and approach to realizing this ambitious goal. While a number of these conclusions derived directly from individual working groups as discussed in chapters 4, 5, 6, and 7, the primary conclusions were arrived at by joint consideration and cut across the groups. Even where a key observation was initiated by a specific working group, its real significance was only established when examined in the context of the other subdisciplines covered by the remaining working groups. This chapter briefly presents each of these major findings with discussion. Their implications for future work are presented in a following chapter.

8.1 Summary Position

A Petaflops computing system will be feasible in two decades and will be important, perhaps even critical, to key applications at that time. Its practicality will rely, in part, on continued advance of the semiconductor industry both in speed enhancement and in cost reduction through improved fabrication processes. While no paradigm shift is required in systems architecture, active latency management will be essential, requiring a very high degree of fine-grain parallelism and the mechanisms to exploit it. One tenable path in device technologies is a mix of technologies including semiconductor for main memory, optics for interprocessor (and perhaps interchip) communications and secondary storage, and possibly superconducting for very high clock rate and very low power processor logic. Effectiveness and applicability will rest on dramatic per device cost reduction and innovative approaches to system software and programming methodologies. Near term studies are required to refine these findings through more detailed examination of system requirements and technology extrapolation.

8.2 Feasibility

Construction of an effective Petaflops computing system will be feasible in about 20 years. This assumes continued rates of growth in key technology areas, advances in others, and development of the necessary software technology. Acceleration of this event is unlikely unless unanticipated breakthroughs occur in areas not considered. Even within this time frame, significant work will be required to turn the raw device technologies into working and useful systems. These predictions are based on extrapolation of SIA projections and consequently incur some uncertainty.

8.3 Broad Potential Use

There are and will be a wide range of applications in science, engineering, economics, and societal information infrastructure and management that will demand Petaflops capability in the near future. Many problems in computer simulation across diverse disciplines will not achieve maturity until systems of this scale become routinely available. Results from such simulations will drive the technologies of the future and feed our understanding of the universe at unprecedented levels of refinement. Nonetheless, the most important applications may be in regimes we can not predict but which will be inspired by these extraordinary capabilities.

8.4 Cost is a Pacing Item

More than any single aspect of a Petaflops initiative, cost will dominate the ultimate viability of such systems and the likely time frame in which they will come in to practical use. If such a system were implemented today using brute-force techniques, it would cost more than a hundred billion dollars. This is prohibitive and will have to be reduced by orders of magnitude to become realizable. Even with aggressive goals of advances to be made, system costs are still expected to fall to between $100 Million and $1 Billion.

8.5 Manageable Reliability

Because of the cost considerations above, a Petaflops system will only be feasible if device integration density places an upper limit on component count of between a hundred thousand and a million. This is within the

Major Findings 155

range of the largest systems being manufactured today. Therefore, it is concluded that the reliability of a Petaflops computing system will be acceptable using known techniques. However, some question remains concerning reliability of on-chip devices as density and wafer size enable chips containing a billion transistors.

8.6 MIMD Model

No fundamental paradigm shift in system architecture is required to achieve this four orders-of-magnitude gain in performance over today's most powerful computing systems. A Non-Uniform Memory Access (NUMA) MIMD structure with possible SIMD elements can provide the key resources and control necessary to provide and organize processing rates on a Petaflops scale. However, many of the details will differ markedly from conventional multiprocessors as will be discussed shortly. Of course, while this finding is considered valid for classes of applications understood today, it is not clear what additional requirements will be imposed by new applications evolving in the context of available Petaflops computing.

8.7 Latency Management and Parallelism

An important characteristic that distinguishes a Petaflops system from conventional MPPs is its wide diameter, which is a measure of the number of clock cycles required for an access request to propagate across the machine. The resulting latency is so substantial that without means for hiding it, system efficiency will suffer unacceptably. Among the means of managing latency are pipelining of communication and single-cycle context switching such as that employed by multithreaded architectures. To achieve this will require the exploitation of vast amounts of parallelism. It is anticipated that many millions of requests will be underway simultaneously, requiring much work in parallel to keep the system processing resources busy. Two feasible alternatives are very low latency systems with a few (1000) very high-performance processors, and systems with millions of processors where almost all accesses are to local memory. For either alternative, latency hiding mechanisms would not be as critical a capability.

8.8 Riding the Semiconductor Technology Wave

The level of investment being applied to technology development by the commercial semiconductor marketplace is substantial and greatly exceeds any augmentation likely from government research programs. Thus, the opportunity to influence expensive development cycles is limited. This situation is exacerbated by the tight coupling between mass production and component cost. Specialty parts become significantly more costly than mass-produced commodity parts of equivalent complexity. Consequently, any initiative to develop a Petaflops computer will have to rely heavily (although not exclusively) on commercially-available components. By leveraging advances that occur as commercial by-products, development costs can be acceptable. But the time to achieve Petaflops will be determined by the "Technology Wave" on which the development is riding.

8.9 Memory

Memory will drive cost as well as many of the architectural decisions. Several of the important findings relate to memory and are grouped in the following subsection*s.

Size

The dominant constituent element of the Petaflops computer is its primary memory. The popular rule-of-thumb is that memory should scale linearly with system peak performance. The assumed implication is that a Petaflops scale system would incorporate a Petabyte of main memory. It was found, however, that for entire classes of scientific and engineering applications, this scaling factor was not valid and that the storage requirement was considerably less. For many cases a scaling factor of the 3/4 root provided an upper bound, with a portion of the probable applications demanding significantly less. As a consequence, the memory size will be between 10 and 40 Terabytes. However, there are instances where more memory is desirable as will be mentioned below.

Bandwidth

To handle the large number of simultaneous transactions required, memory bandwidth will have to be significantly increased with respect to memory size over today's standards. The actual on-chip memory bandwidth is very high and it is only its interface to external devices that inhibits its use. New memory organizations that overcome this limitation will be essential in the Petaflops system design.

Global Name Space

A common name space across the machine, while not required by some applications, is a valuable means of simplifying programming, implementing resource management software, and (through hardware support) minimizing overhead for fine-grain remote access requests. In this last case, where fine-grain parallelism is required for scalability, software overhead in managing address space translation is not tenable as it often would overwhelm the useful work to be performed. Support of a global name space is important for both human and machine effectiveness.

Petabyte Computer

A separate although related topic is a class of computers that emphasizes memory more than performance. Many information management applications of the future may be more dependent on availability of main memory than on peak performance. This is really a different class of computer than the Petaflops computer which is the focus of this workshop. But it is a conclusion of the workshop that memory intensive systems will play a significant role.

8.10 Software Paradigm Shift

Tha Achilles' heel of exploiting massively parallelism is that the programming methodologies being used and the resource management software are completely inadequate to the challenge. An entirely new programming paradigm may be essential to the effective use of these systems, and it must extend beyond the central computer to incorporate semantics that deal with the information infrastructure in which such systems will be embedded. One area for hope is that complicated compile time analysis algorithms (only at the fringe of being possible due to their intense compute requirements) will be facilitated greatly by the availability of a Petaflops capability.

8.11 Merging of Technologies

Device technologies of the future may exhibit more disparate characteristics that the rather exclusive and homogeneous use of semiconductor technology today. It was concluded that the merging of several technologies would give a stronger Petaflops system than attempting to implement it from only one basic technology. This is similar to fabricating structural elements such as steel reinforced concrete from distinct materials: the concrete provides superior compressive force while the internal steel rods yield exceptional tensile strength. Likewise, superconductive devices will provide extremely high-speed logic, and very low power optics will give the system the necessary internal bandwidth, while semiconductor technology will be used for the high-density main memory.

8.12 A Role for Superconductivity

As indicated above, a surprise to many of the workshop participants was the plausible application of superconducting technology to the challenge of implementing a Petaflops computer. The improvement in clock speed of perhaps two orders of magnitude over semiconductor speeds will be important to cost-effective system production. But the low power requirements compared with those anticipated for semiconductor processors may be crucial. This being the case, the relatively low support activity for cryogenic digital technology in the U.S. is a topic of some concern.

8.13 Optical Logic Unlikely

A disappointment to many participants was the unavoidable conclusion that for general-purpose computing, optical technology is unlikely to provide a path to high-density, high-speed, low-latency logic that can be used in the Petaflops computers. While there may be a role for such devices for very specialized hardwired computing systems, their use as constituent elements of the class of systems targeted is not tenable.

9 Issues and Implications

The results and consequences of this historic workshop go beyond the primary findings presented in the previous chapter. A number of important issues were considered that have direct bearing on the potential of Petaflops-scale computing systems and possible directions of future research leading to this achievement. These issues are presented in this chapter and their implications discussed.

9.1 Why Consider Petaflops Now?

The aggregate networked compute power in the United States today is estimated to be between 10 and 100 Teraflops; by the end of the decade it is expected to reach a Petaflops. The focus of this workshop was to determine the means of implementing a single computer capable of more performance than all the computers on Earth put together. Far from being treated as unduly premature or even superfluous, the goal was dealt with seriously and in earnest by all participants. Why?

The fundamental issue driving this workshop is that the stakes are too high for the U.S. to leave this future technology in the hands of other nations. It may be that dealing with the Petaflops question now will not have a demonstrable effect on the computing industry for some years. But, when the technology begins to have impact, the ground work will have been laid years in advance, and only those nations having previously invested in the underlying enabling technologies will be positioned to play a commanding role in its exploitation.

Results from this workshop indicate that the U.S. is already lagging in specific technologies that may be crucial to Petaflops computing. The U.S. is no longer the premier producer of high-density memory technology. Yet, one of the key findings is that memory will be *the* major component determining both the capability and the cost of such systems. A nation that cannot produce competitive high-performance memory will not be able to compete in the Petaflops market. Another example is cryogenic Josephson Junction technology. Once the world leader, the U.S. has been displaced by Japan in the production and application of this technology and now we have seen that it may be crucial to low power, high-speed processing at the Petaflops level.

This workshop constituted a deliberate and concerted effort to determine the critical capabilities required to take a leadership role and to establish now an initial path in that direction. An open issue at the beginning of this workshop was the merit of the subject itself. The implications of the workshop findings is that not only does the topic warrant consideration and is timely, but that early action must be taken in the areas of devices, architecture, and system software to ensure U.S. capability into the next century. Therefore, an important implication of the findings of the workshop is the legitimization of the discipline of Petaflops computing systems.

9.2 Role of a Petaflops Computer

The stereotypical image of a supercomputer and its small user community working on a narrow range of scientific applications in the depths of some laboratory machine room is unlikely to be mirrored by a Petaflops system some years hence. It is much more likely that such a facility will ordinarily be shared by many users distributed throughout the country on a wide array of applications and information support services. Indeed, it has been proposed that a Petaflops system may not be a single computer but rather a more loosely integrated confederation of computers. Such a confederation can cooperate on the execution of one or more very large programs, but more frequently engage in the support of a larger user base performing a number of smaller problems by time-slicing and space-slicing available resources. The issue is not one of wasting precious high-end resources on less important smaller problems. Rather, key to the success of Petaflops computers is broadening their relevance across a much wider user base so that their market share becomes sufficient to amortize their development costs across a greater installed base. Also, the class of applications demanding high performance will extend well beyond the classical scientific problems to include general information infrastructure and management services. It is possible to imagine tens of thousands of users simultaneously accessing a single information archive. Visual presentation of complex data through real time interactive animation may become the norm demanding this scale of capacity. The applications working group and software technology working group considered many other means of employing Petaflops systems. But the overall conclusion is that the role of computers must and will diversify as opportunities permit new mass-appeal applications and economics demand cost-effective implementation of Petaflops computers through mass production and markets.

9.3 Side-effect Products

It is assumed that a computer, no matter how powerful or how far in the future, cannot exceed some magic dollar figure (normalized for inflation) in customer cost or otherwise it becomes inaccessible for procurement. For purposes of discussion, this figure was fixed at a level of $100M. This sets an upper bound on the cost of devices and subsystems comprising the Petaflops computer. Also, assuming an approximately linear scaling of cost to performance and the general scalability of the subsystem ensembles making up the Petaflops machine, then a system in the cost range of a high-end workstation today would deliver a large fraction of a Teraflops. Thus, a spin-off of the Petaflops research would be workstations more powerful than this Nation's largest computer today. While this may seem farfetched, it is consistent with experience. A high-end lap top today equals or exceeds the performance of the largest mainframe computers around 1970. A high-end workstation today equals the performance of a CRAY 1 in 1975. Should we be so surprised that this relative performance advance may repeat itself? More seriously, even today, an ever increasing percentage of the scientific computing workload is being migrated from the supercomputer to the desktop workstation due to their relatively high availability. The implications of Teraflops capability at everyone's finger tips is very exciting and should revolutionize scientific discovery.

9.4 Impact of Exotic Technologies

The preeminence of semiconductor technology over alternative possibilities has limited the availability of R&D funds for such interesting devices as cryogenic and optical digital components. In relative terms, funding for cryogenics has been shrinking with respect to investment in semiconductor fabrication. Optical technology has avoided starvation only because of the impact of long distance fiber optic cables for communications and mass market optical disks for storage of consumer music and video images. And it is expected that semiconductor technology will continue to play an important role over the next two decades including support for Petaflops systems. But, in spite of the dominance of semiconductor devices now and into the future, the workshop found that semiconductor technology will probably not be adequate and that these more exotic technologies are likely to be in the critical path to success.

Two key observations were made during the workshop that altered the perspective of many in participants in considering the right mix of technologies making up a Petaflops computer. JJ technology would appear to provide a viable path to clock rates of between one and two orders of magnitude beyond current speeds. More importantly, superconducting devices consume very little power and therefore dissipate only a small amount of heat. The amount of power required to run an all-semiconductor machine may be prohibitive. A processing element comprising JJ devices may be an essential means of making Petaflops computing practical. Also, it became clear that the cooling systems even in the worst case (the present situation) are tolerable and would not unduly burden the support infrastructure. Furthermore, little work has been done to make cooling of superconducting elements more efficient, but the problem should yield to concerted effort. One weakness of cryogenics is the lack of a satisfactory high-density memory device.

Optical technology can produce pulses measured in femtoseconds (10^{-15} seconds). But photons do not easily interact and it became clear that logic gates derived from purely optical means were unlikely to provide the basis for a Petaflops computer. Fiber optics, on the other hand, exhibit exceptional bandwidth that will be critical in handling the enormous message traffic between very high speed processors and the Terabytes of global memory. This is certainly going to be true across boards and perhaps even between integrated circuits, although there is some controversy on this point. In addition, the massive amount of archival information to be stored for retrieval in the emerging globally-accessible depositories may demand the densities that in the future will be provided optically. It was also noted that optical communication channels make good interfaces to superconducting circuits because of their low thermal conductivity properties.

The implication of these findings is that a possible Petaflops computing system may comprise substantial elements of all three technologies.

More to the point, it may be essential that all three technologies be incorporated to realize a viable system at the intended performance level. Therefore, some investment of these two exotic technologies in the immediate future would be prudent, if for no other reason than to ascertain their true potential in meeting the needs of a Petaflops system.

9.5 Performance Versus Efficiency

Historically, computer performance has been measured in peak throughput, an often unattainable upper bound. Sustained performance gives a somewhat more realistic measure of behavior, albeit for specific applications. But, for applications that are constantly evolving, development time can dominate the "time to solution." This can be very different from the few minutes to few hours of execution time used when an application code finally is debugged and optimized. The real cost to the end user seeking a solution to such problems is the days, weeks, or months of program development time required.

A Petaflops computer, if anything, will extend greatly the distributed nature of the computing resources and so significantly aggravate the apparent difficulties that the time to solution could be extended to an unacceptable degree. A fundamental implication of this trend is that it may be necessary to rethink what is important to emphasize in system design and be prepared to trade lower sustained performance for shorter program development time. This is a difficult mind set to establish as we emerge from the recent supercomputer era. But it may be necessary if Petaflops systems are to be of widespread use in the real world.

9.6 Programming Paradigms

It has become mandatory, in light of the comments above, to consider the question of programming paradigms. The HPCC program is developing message-passing and data-parallel models and languages for programming scalable parallel computers up to the Teraflops performance level. While these methods have yielded successful execution of some large and important problems, these successes have come at the expense of arduous programming efforts. And, these efforts have been made even more difficult because the languages employed simply do not provide the expressive power required to adequately harness such complex systems and match their resources to the demands of ever increasing dynamic and irregular applications.

The reluctance of the scientific programming community to relinquish Fortran is slowly giving way to a recognition that a richer methodology is essential to effective exploitation of massive parallelism. Even with this emerging realization, there are few strong alternative candidates and less concurrence on the best approach. While we do not know what the language is, we can put forth some of the things it must do. It must enable all of the application parallelism, in its many possible forms, to be exposed to the underlying system (hardware and software) implicitly or explicitly. It must depict the abstract data movement of an algorithm and task concurrency and interdependencies such that compile-time and run-time resource management strategies can perform process scheduling and placement in a near optimal fashion. It must allow very high level descriptions of tasks to be performed to minimize the amount of detail required by the programmer. It must support diverse parallel execution models permitting mixes of styles seamlessly in a single application program. Perhaps by the time the first Petaflops computers emerge, such a language will have evolved.

9.7 U.S. Capabilities in Memory Fabrication

A basic finding of the workshop was that memory will constitute a major part of the Petaflops computing system and impose the foremost component of cost. An important issue is whether or not a country intending to be a dominant force in the Petaflops market can do so without also having a commanding lead in DRAM and SRAM fabrication and manufacturing. One observation is that the U.S. is no longer the leader in memory production, but is a major producer of computing systems. Therefore, it may be argued, a similar balance could exist 20 years from now. The opposing view is based on two observations about the Petaflops systems. First, it is expected that the Petaflops system will be significantly more memory intensive relatively speaking with respect to processor and communication logic than systems today. This is because achieving the required aggregate processor throughput is a function of both increased logic density and increased clock speed while memory size is helped by density improvements alone. As a consequence, for Petaflops computers with the same ratio of processor speed memory as present computers, the relative proportion of the machine will become more heavily biased to memory. Thus the impact of having to rely on foreign memory may be prohibitive. But perhaps the second reason is more important. At least one of the three architecture concepts considered by the workshop requires that both memory and processor logic be integrated on a single die to maximize memory to processor bandwidth. Memory implementation methodology is evolving into a specialization that does not track advances in logic. Therefore, in order to implement high density, high-speed combined processor/memory modules, a source must be skilled in the state of the art in both technologies.

9.8 Special Widgets, Where to Invest

While the focus of Petaflops system design will be the integration of commercially available components, there may be requirements for modules derived expressly for use within such systems. However, the design of even a few custom integrated circuits may so overwhelm the development cycle that it could become the most significant part of the system realization. Also, the cost per component for custom parts used only in such high-end systems may become a disproportionately large cost factor. This is an issue because avoiding the use of parts not commercially available may severely constrain design choices and limit system effectiveness. This issue was left open because there were proponents of both views. To resolve this question will require detailed analysis of the trade-offs including the resource demands of a representative workload.

9.9 A Range of Architectures

No single architecture was adopted, but three were considered that varied in terms of processor granularity, clock speed, and latency. The reason for this lack of convergence was not failure to reach consensus but rather a recognition that there are several viable approaches to be considered. Until greater certainty is possible in terms of technology capability and best performance to cost, it is advisable to examine a range of alternatives. The processor speeds assumed range from a Teraflops at the high end to 10 Gigaflops at the low end, per processor. At the high end, communication latency is assumed to be low, and accesses to memory banks are overlapped. This would be a uniform access, shared memory machine. The other extreme has memory and processors on the same chips providing very good local memory access and high system-wide memory bandwidth, although of a local nature. Such a system may not support a shared-memory model through hardware, although it is possible. The final architecture considered was the middle ground of on the order of 10,000 processors capable of multithreading to hide latency and sharing the global memory.

The three architectures vary both in the demands they impose on technology and in the class of applications that would be best supported by each. For example, the classic form of data-parallel applications with regular and local accesses dominating might be performed to best advantage on a machine where local memory is most accessible. Applications with somewhat limited parallelism would be most suited to the high-end processors with low latency to global memory and fewer processors. Irregular and time-varying problems with abundant parallelism could benefit most easily from the middle system, one whose thread scheduling adapts to conditions of variable latency.

The workshop actually considered a single heterogeneous system comprised of one of each architecture such that the total performance was a Petaflops, but each constituent computer was some number of hundreds of Teraflops. This was based on the expectation that for any single problem, at least one of the three machines would be well suited to its needs. This then would yield a better performance to cost across a diverse workload than any single one of the architectures scaled to a Petaflops. Other heterogeneous structures are possible also, and should be considered in detail as part of follow-on studies.

9.10 Far-side Architectures

It was found that a tenable approach to Petaflops architecture could be derived from a balance of known processor and memory architecture techniques combined with somewhat less conventional but still understood latency hiding techniques. Consequently, with the limited time available, no additional architectural structures were considered. This may, in fact, prove to be the right course of action in the long run. But it is not out of the question that a more radical departure in parallel architecture might bring Petaflops performance within reach in far less than the 20 years estimated. This is particularly true for domain-specific architectures targeted toward a restricted class of applications. Cellular automata, systolic arrays, and associative memory are all examples of architectures that perform a narrow set of operations at extremely high rates. With the merging of processing in memory, a mix of the above might be possible that permits a class of general computing structures exploiting the performance benefits of each. While highly speculative, some thought needs to be given to possible alternatives that conceivably could greatly shorten the time to realizing Petaops (if not Petaflops) systems.

9.11 Latency Hiding Techniques May Help Smaller Machines

It was recognized that as effort is invested in developing a Petaflops computer, some of technology and techniques devised may have value in other sectors of the computer market. It was mentioned previously that this might be essential for the larger systems to be economically viable. Also, the possibility for a Teraflops workstation is an exciting prospect. Another is the recognition that the latency-hiding methods devised for the Petaflops systems may be entirely appropriate for the less demanding systems of tens of processors or even uniprocessors. The key characteristic is that these methods are run-time adaptive and will not suffer the sort of performance degradation being experienced by High-Q processors with caches attempting to run large scientific problems with data exhibiting low locality.

9.12 Long versus Short Latency Machines

While much time was spent considering large diameter machines, an alternative that has worked well in the past was also considered. Short-latency machines have significant advantages over long-latency machines in terms of programming and efficiency. Supercomputers such as the CRAY 3 achieve much of their performance from a combination of very high clock rate and very short transmission distances between modules. Assuming density continues to increase, it is possible to imagine very small machines with short diameters. This would provide a true shared-memory system with all resources equally accessible. The engineering challenges to achieving this are formidable but merit further inquiry.

9.13 SIA Predictions

An important contribution to the workshop was the baseline of industry projections for the growth of semiconductors. It is important to note that the finding of a potential Petaflops computing system in 20+ years is based on raw extrapolation of the SIA predictions. This is dangerous not only because the detailed work to extend these projections has not been done, but because it is understood that new quantum effects will begin to take hold beyond the levels of integration dealt with by the SIA studies. Therefore at lithographic resolutions finer than 0.1 microns, it is unclear how the semiconductor technology will evolve. The implication is that there is a degree of uncertainty in the workshop findings above and beyond ordinary projections, and planners have to be cognizant of the risks based solely on this study.

9.14 I/O Scaling

While the focus of architectural considerations were on processor speeds and memory bandwidth, another area of importance is input and output mechanisms to secondary storage and networks. It was recognized that I/O would scale less than linearly with system performance and might not prove as difficult to achieve as some of the other challenging system requirements. Nonetheless, given recent history with I/O bottlenecks on current MPP systems, the issue warrants a deeper examination. For example, just filling the main memory of such a computer imposes a substantial burden on the I/O subsystem. Suppose one wants to checkpoint the memory contents just once an hour and the memory comprises approximately 30 Terabytes as proposed by the Applications and Architectures working groups. This alone would impose an average demand of 10 Gigabytes per second bandwidth. But, in fact, one would not want this overhead to be more than a small fraction of the overall system usage, or about five percent. Then the required I/O bandwidth increases to about 200 Gigabytes per second. Today's disk drives might provide 10 Mbits per second peak. To absorb the checkpointing data rate on such a system would require on the order of 100,000 disk drives. This is an imposing number and makes clear that Petaflops systems as being envisioned require detailed consideration of the implications for I/O and secondary storage support infrastructure. Moreover, the problem is exacerbated if the main memory is actually in the range of a Petabyte as some futuristic applications were thought to require, increasing demand by more than another order of magnitude.

10
Recommendations and Conclusions

10.1 Recommendations for Near-Term Initiatives

While the workshop assembled a highly qualified group of experts, many details were left unresolved due to the limited duration of the workshop. Prior to major initiatives being undertaken, it will be necessary to engage in short near-term studies to sharpen the findings of this book. These studies are necessary to better understand the balance of resources required by the applications to use such systems and to establish a more precise projection of technology trends for the next decade and a half. The recommendations follow below.

Superconducting Technology

Identify key areas of research in cryogenic device technology for which a small amount of funding in the near term will significantly reduce uncertainty about the potential of this technology to contribute to a Petaflops computer implementation. Specific topics include:
   Superconducting memory for buffers, registers, and cache
   Clock speeds of devices likely to be achieved
   Optical connect to external world
   Densities likely to be achieved
   Ways of lowering cooling overhead.

Scaled-up Applications Resource Requirements

Define applications for the architecture and software communities in an implementation independent manner. This will lead to a more complete understanding of the resource demands imposed by applications including memory requirements for applications running at Petaflops levels. This needs to be done across a broad range of applications. Also important is the study of available parallelism and granularity of irregular and dynamic applications and their implications on system resource management mechanisms.

A Future Application Scenario

Explore possible resource demands for future applications enabled by Petaflops/Petabyte computers. These might include full immersion virtual reality environments used for the scientific and engineering communities, as well as for more general community access to nationwide information and processing resources.

Detailed Architectures

Conduct a study leading to a complete sketch of one or more Petaflops computers. This study should include primary resource requirements and first-order behavior characteristics. From this should come an understanding of clock speeds, number of processors, aggregate required interprocessor and memory bandwidth, latencies, level of parallelism, and pacing items in device technology.

Extend SIA Projections

Extend SIA projections beyond 0.1 microns to provide better predictions of semiconductor technology capabilities in 20+ years. This is important to bounding the uncertainty about the viability of certain approaches. These projections should be considered for both processor logic and memory devices as recent evidence suggests they are following different growth and scaling paths.

Programming Methodologies

Engage in an objective review of possible programming methodologies and resource management techniques with the goal of focusing on approaches that go beyond HPCC models and may contribute to Petaflops computer usability. Through such an examination, some over-the-horizon questions may be identified which currently are obscured by short-term considerations.

Alternative Concepts and Approaches

Survey emerging fields and approaches that may be relevant but which were not examined in detail at the workshop. The goal here is to make certain that possibilities are not overlooked, even if the ideas are incipient and difficult to evaluate. It is from such areas that unanticipated breakthroughs occasionally come, dramatically altering the course of technology evolution. Areas of consideration might include molecular computing, neural nets, optical logic for special-purpose applications,

Recommendations and Conclusions 173

machine self-programming means, and other possibilities of a radical (and high risk) nature not considered in any detail at this workshop.

Alternative Architectural Approaches

Include, among the more radical areas to be explored, alternative architecture paradigms. Upon examination of the known data, the workshop clearly concluded that modifications of conventional approaches would suffice to enable Petaflops capability. But, implicit in this seminal finding is the caveat that we have to wait 20 years. It is conceivable that a different, unconventional approach to computer architecture might provide a different development path converging on Petaflops performance much earlier, at least for domain-specific workloads. Prior to starting a substantial research program, all the currently known possibilities should be exposed for consideration, even if not pursued to any extent.

Inexpensive Teraflops Machines

As noted in chapter 9, a side effect of developing an economically viable Petaflops computer technology is the possibility of cost competitive Teraflops systems in a range that may make one available to every computational scientist. It is appropriate even now to engage in a design study to explore the architecture and device technology issues related to Teraflops workstations. These may become as important in the overall computing environment as the large Petaflops central computers.

Review Progress

If the previous recommendations in total or significant part are acted upon, it may be appropriate to reassess our understanding of the potential for achieving a Petaflops system. This might be appropriate in a couple of years as new results are produced. The precise nature and form of such a review should be determined nearer to the event because it may depend on the consequences of the updated findings during the intervening period.

10.2 Concluding Observations

Petaflops computing system will be feasible and can be very useful. Therefore, it will be developed. The key questions are: when?, by whom (which nation)?, and how will it be implemented and used? The tentative answers derived from this workshop are a mix of optimism and caution; optimism about the ultimate potential of such systems currently beyond human experience, caution about the challenges that separate today's speculations from tomorrow's reality. The breadth of issues explored revealed important considerations for technology planners and research policy makers in the near future.

When?

Device and system technology will make possible the realization of Petaflops computing systems in 20 to 25 years if current technology trends continue and specific enabling technologies are matured. This assumes that a Petaflops architecture will be of the form as described in this book using multiprocessing principles and structures. It is conceivable, but not anticipated, that a dramatically different approach and architecture might yield equivalent capability in a shorter time-frame.

By whom?

The Petaflops computer will be developed, marketed, and applied by the nation(s) with a leading semiconductor industry; a dominant high-speed, high-density semiconductor industrial fabrication capability; an aggressive, advanced device technologies applied research program in optics and cryogenic devices; and a sophisticated software technology methodology and infrastructure.

Usage?

If targeted only to Grand Challenge-scale applications used in a few institutions, such systems will be largely unusable, unaffordable, and unlikely to be realized. The impact of such systems, constrained in this manner, may be insufficient to warrant the necessary expenditures.

However, the Petaflops computer can be targeted to both the growing scientific and engineering communities with strong industrial very high-end application and to the broader information management mass-market community of the future. With advanced rapid-programming methodologies and integration as part of the national information infrastructure, the Petaflops computer will be economically viable and used directly or indirectly by millions of information-action driven consumers.

The impact of such systems, made broadly applicable to a nation's socioeconomic needs, would be immense and merit the long term R&D investment required.

Long Lead to Research-derived Products

Long lead time research is essential if we are to be positioned competitively when Petaflops capability becomes feasible. Applied research starting in the near future will be necessary to be competitive in the 15 to 20 year time frame, even though the products of such advanced work may not have short-term impact. To make a long-term commitment to stay the course requires strong confidence in the chosen path. A first step in that direction is the reduction in uncertainties remaining after the workshop. The objective is to narrow the scope of possible paths, minimizing the risk of each, and eliminating high risk, low reward directions. But ultimately, risk is an intrinsic property of any research and must be factored in to the research program by sponsoring multiple projects exploring alternate approaches.

Leverage Mainstream Hardware and Software Technology

High-performance computing must become mainstream in order to leverage investment by the industrial and commercial sectors in enabling hardware and software technology. Only through the participation of major independent software vendors (ISVs) in high-performance computing will the development of mass market software benefit the future application of the Petaflops computer. This means that systems must be made compatible with commercial software, and programming models must be available to ISVs to permit them to enter the parallel programming world with high confidence in commercial success. Similarly, Petaflops computer architecture will be dependent on components designed primarily for the mass market such as workstations and networking. Those rare instances when specialty parts will be incorporated will be strategically defined for their pivotal role in realizing Petaflops capability. Otherwise, commodity components, even if suboptimal for a particular purpose, will prove superior in performance to cost and development time.

Value Beyond Applications

Benefits from the development of the Petaflops computer will exceed the worth implied by the sum of the applications that could make use of it. It will drive creativity, technology, and capabilities essential to U.S. competitiveness in multiple arenas in ways which cannot be foreseen but which will be of extreme value and importance.

Intellectual Synergism

An important immediate consequence of this workshop beyond the greater understanding achieved of Petaflops computing systems was the extraordinary synergism and cross fertilization of ideas that occurred among some of this nation's major contributors to computer science and industry. Rarely have that many scientists across a broad range of interrelated disciplines been harnessed for such a length of time to focus on such a far reaching topic. All participants felt they came away from the experience with more than they had brought.

A Attendee List

David Barkai (NASA)
Doc Bedard (National Security Agency)
Larry Bergman (Jet Propulsion Laboratory)
Tom Blank (MasPar Computer Corporation)
Paul Boudreaux (National Security Agency)
Joe Brewer (Westinghouse Electric Corporation)
Tim Brice (NASA/Jet Propulsion Laboratory)
Bill Carlson (Supercomputing Research Center)
Tony Chan (University of California Los Angeles)
Terry Cole (Jet Propulsion Laboratory)
George Cotter (National Security Agency)
Seymour Cray (Cray Computer Corporation)
John Dorband (NASA-GSFC)
Dwight Duston (Ballistic Missile Defense Organization)
Walter Ermler (U. S. Department of Energy)
John Feo (Lawrence Livermore National Laboratory)
Jim Fischer (NASA-GSFC)
Geoffrey Fox (Northeast Parallel Architectures Center)
Bruce Fryxell (NASA-GSFC)
Dennis Gannon (Indiana University)
Ed Giorgio (U. S. Department of Defense)
James Glimm (State University of New York, Stony Brook)
Andrew Grimshaw (University of Virginia)
Bert Halstead (Digital Equipment Corporation)
Michael Heath (University of Illinois)
Alan Huang (AT & T Bell Laboratories)
Pete Kogge (IBM Corporation)
Norm Kreisman (U. S. Department of Energy)
Carl Kukkonen (NASA/Jet Propulsion Laboratory)
Monica Lam (Stanford University)
Sing Lee (University of California San Diego)
Kostya Likharev (State University of New York)
Lou Lome (Ballistic Missile Defense Organization)
Jacob Maizel (National Institutes of Health)
Mary Maloney (California Institute of Technology)
James McGraw (HPCC National Coordination Office)
Piyush Mehrotra (NASA/ICASE)

Paul Messina (California Institute of Technology)
A. Ray Miller (National Security Agency)
John Neff (University of Colorado)
Steve Nelson (Cray Research, Inc.)
Michelle O'Connell (NASA/CESDIS)
Cherri Pancake (Oregon State University)
Greg Papadopoulos (Thinking Machines Corporation)
Steven Pei (AT & T Bell Laboratories)
John Peterson (NASA/Jet Propulsion Laboratory)
John Pinkston (National Security Agency)
James C. T. Pool (California Institute of Technology)
John Przybysz (Westinghouse Electric Corporation)
Justin Rattner (Intel Supercomputers)
Coke Reed (Supercomputing Research Center)
Daniel Reed (University of Illinois Urbana-Champaign)
Joel Saltz (University of Maryland)
Rob Schreiber (NASA/RIACS)
Arnold Silver (TRW)
Burton Smith (Tera Computer Company)
Paul H. Smith (NASA HQ)
Martin Sokoloski (Science and Technology Corporation)
Thomas Sterling (USRA CESDIS)
Rick Stevens (Argonne National Laboratory)
Paul Stolorz (NASA/Jet Propulsion Laboratory)
Harold Stone (IBM Corporation)
Francis Sullivan (Supercomputing Research Center)
Bob Westervelt (Harvard University)
Richard Zippel (Cornell University)

Bibliography

[Covick:90a] Covick, L. A., and Sando, M. K. *J. Comput. Chem.*, 11:1151, 1990.

[Feldman:88a] Feldman, M., Esener, S., Guest, C., and Lee, S. H. "Comparison between optical and electrical interconnects based on power and speed considerations," *Applied Optics*, 27(9):1742–1751, May 1988.

[Harrison:93a] Harrison, R. J., and Kendall, R. A. *Theoret. Chim. Acta*, 84:489, 1993.

[Hunter:90a] Hunter, S., Kiamilev, F., Esener, S., Parthenopoulos, D., and Rentzepis, P. "Potentials of two-photon based 3-d optical memories for high performance computing," *Applied Optics*, 29(14):2058–2066, May 1990.

[Likharev:93a] Likharev, K. *The New Superconducting Electronics*, pages 423–452. Kluver, Dordrecht, 1993.

[Likharev:94a] Likharev, K. K., and Semenov, V. K. *IEEE Trans. Appl. Supercond.*, 1:3–28, March 1994.

[Messina:93d] Messina, P., and Sterling, T., editors. *System Software and Tools for High-Performance Computing Environments*. SIAM, Philadelphia, 1993. Caltech Report CCSF-35b.

[Mulliken:81a] Mulliken, R. S., and Ermler, W. C. *Polyatomic Molecules: Results of ab Initio Calculations*. Academic Press, New York, 1981.

[Parish:90a] Parish, T. "Crystal clear storage," *BYTE*, pages 283–288, November 1990.

[Ross:94a] Ross, R. B., Ermler, W. C., Kern, C. W., and Pitzer, R. M. "Modelling bulk berylium," *Supercomputer*, 1994. Accepted for Publication.

[SIA:93a] "Semiconductor technology workshop conclusions," 1993. Semiconductor Industry Association (roadmap table appears on page 6).

[Smith:93a] *Workshop and Conference on Grand Challenge Applications and Software Technology*, May 1993. Pittsburgh, Pennsylvania (GCW-0593).

[Tsang:90a] Tsang, D. Z. "Optical interconnections in digital systems—status and prospects," *Optics and Photonics News*, 1(10):23–29, 1990.

Scientific and Engineering Computation
Janusz Kowalik, editor

Data-Parallel Programming on MIMD Computers, Philip J. Hatcher and Michael J. Quinn, 1991

Unstructured Scientific Computation on Scalable Multiprocessors, edited by Piyush Mehrotra, Joel Saltz, and Robert Voigt, 1992

Parallel Computational Fluid Dynamics: Implementations and Results, edited by Horst D. Simon, 1992

Enterprise Integration Modeling: Proceedings of the First International Conference, edited by Charles J. Petrie, Jr., 1992

The High Performance Fortran Handbook, Charles H. Koelbel, David B. Loveman, Robert S. Schreiber, Guy L. Steele Jr., and Mary E. Zosel, 1994

Using MPI: Portable Parallel Programming with the Message-Passing Interface, William Gropp, Ewing Lusk, and Anthony Skjellum, 1994

PVM: Parallel Virtual Machine—A Users' Guide and Tutorial for Networked Parallel Computing, Al Geist, Adam Beguelin, Jack Dongarra, Weicheng Jiang, Robert Mancheck, and Vaidy Sunderam, 1994

Enabling Technologies for Petaflops Computing, Thomas Sterling, Paul Messina, and Paul H. Smith, 1995